SHORT CUTS

INTRODUCTIONS TO FILM STUDIES

NEW CHINESE CINEMA

CHALLENGING REPRESENTATIONS

SHEILA CORNELIUS
with
IAN HAYDN SMITH

WALLFLOWER

LONDON and NEW YORK

A Wallflower Paperback

First published in Great Britain in 2002 by Wallflower Press
5 Pond Street, Hampstead, London, NW3 2PN
www.wallflowerpress.co.uk

A catalogue record for this book is available from the British Library

ISBN 1 903364 13 2

Book Design by Rob Bowden Design

Printed in Great Britain by Antony Rowe Ltd, Chippenham, Wiltshire

CONTENTS

LIST OF ILLUSTRATIONS

ACKNOWLEDGEMENTS

I would like to thank Huang Wen of Goldsmiths College, Lillian Chia of Westminster University and Ann Gold of Morley College for their encouragement and inspiration. Thanks also to my ex-colleagues and students at Maris Stella High School, Singapore, who taught me so much about Chinese culture, especially Annie Cheong and my former student Zhang Jiajun. I am also grateful to my friend Dr Linda Bilton for her support, my colleagues in London for their interest and company at screenings, and in particular to Dawn Young for practical help and advice. Finally, thank you to my husband Roy, for coming to my classes and watching so many Chinese films with me.

The publishers would like to thank Ian Haydn Smith for all his work in the preparation of this book.

INTRODUCTION

The intention of this book is to help students and those with an interest in Chinese cinema understand it by placing it within a social and political context. Film writers have made Chinese films more accessible in recent years, attracting audiences outside that normally found at film festivals and art-house cinemas; their approaches make up the canon of film debate, influenced, in particular, by structuralism, semiotics, feminism, psychoanalysis, neo-Marxism, postmodernism and postcolonialism. With this introduction, students may participate more fully with some knowledge of the society that produced the films and the contexts in which they were made.

This approach to the study of Chinese films is particularly appropriate because the traditional role of artists in China – including writers and film-makers – has been to comment on society. Film representations, however, reflect not just the experiences and beliefs of film-makers, but the views of those who make decisions about what is permitted to be shown. It is this area which the book seeks to explore and, in its focus on the films of Fifth and Sixth Generation mainland directors, discuss the ways in which those who disagreed with 'official' opinions gave expression to their experience on film.

In the mid-1980s a new wave of Chinese films made an immediate impression on critics at international film festivals. Symbolic use of colour, landscape, and objects combined to explore complex themes, questioning the fundamentals of historical and contemporary Chinese culture. This book aims to explain the background to these developments and set them in their social and historical context. It will do so by examining the 'search for roots' films that emerged from China in the aftermath of the Cultural Revolution (1966–76) and charting the developments from these 'beginnings' to the rise of more contemporary 'Sixth Generation' underground directors, whose themes embrace social dislocation and the disaffection of urban youth.

Chapter 1 presents an overview of the changes that swept through China throughout the twentieth century and looks at how the West perceived the Chinese through film and literature. Mao Zedong changed the course of Chinese history by imposing a modern belief system on a society hidebound by tradition. Mao, the idealistic son of a 'middle peasant', observed at close hand in his youth the oppressions of weak government, a rigid class system and foreign depredations. After a struggle to gain an education for himself and win popular support, at first allying his young Chinese Communist Party (CCP) with the Soviet Union for finance and technical aid, he developed the film industry as an 'educational' tool to bring news of the Party's achievements and their aspirations to a vast and illiterate population.

We shall see how the West had portrayed China in film and literature in a negative light since the early 1900s. These portrayals were closely related to the history of relations with China, the recruitment of cheap labour and the growth of Chinatowns, particularly with respect to Britain and America. Recent images retain some of the characteristics of early stereotypes, despite the filmic portrayals of the new 'transnational' directors. Zhang Yimou's *To Live* (1994) (film titles in the original Chinese are given the the filmography) presented one family's account of their attempts to survive the political and social upheavals of Mao's reign. A contrast to the propagandist films of previous decades, its criticism of government policies resulted in strict censure from the government.

Chapter 2 examines how the Fifth Generation came into being and how their style of film-making attempted to avoid the restrictions of state censorship. Following Mao's death, the Beijing Film Academy re-opened its doors, and from the first graduating classes rose a number of directors who would have a profound impact on Chinese cinema. Directors such as Chen Kaige, Tian Zhuangzhuang and Zhang Yimou all shared a common purpose: to express their pain and question a culture which had seemingly destroyed tradition, disrupted the education of millions, and taken the lives of countless thousands of ordinary Chinese. Using popular forms and genres and exploiting the potential for ambiguity inherent in the moving image, the films of this period achieved a standard of excellence that was soon recognised in the West. These films also attracted the attention of the authoritarian government established in 1949 under Mao and were heavily criticised for exposing the regime – and indeed the whole of the Chinese nation – to the critical gaze of the West. The institutions for tight censorship controls persisted after Mao's death and the fall of the Gang of Four (political extremists who were blamed for the worst excesses of the Cultural Revolution). The right to representation was then strongly contested by the Fifth Generation directors.

Protected to some extent by international acclaim, and the financial benefits to the industry of foreign funding, the directors who continued film-making in China adopted strategies which sought, in turn, to appease the Party, fool the censors, and negotiate the representation of reality as they saw and experienced it. Tian Zhuangzhuang's film *The Blue Kite* (1993) presented an alternative account of the effect of see-sawing political campaigns and directives on the lives of 'ordinary' Chinese. The telling portrait of a society tyrannised by a well-meaning but misguided and divided government ensured it was banned in its home country.

Chapter 3 looks at how the visual and narrative style of the Fifth Generation films differed from its predecessors. Acknowledged as the first film of the new wave is *Yellow Earth* (1984), directed by Chen Kaige with cinematography by Zhang Yimou and released from the Xian Studio. One of a series of films set in remote areas of the Chinese countryside, where the national tendency to stick to rigid traditions was at its strongest, *Yellow Earth* portrays the bleak landscape of the Loess Plateau region of China, traversed by the Yellow River which traditionally symbolises the nation. It depicts the efforts of a young revolutionary soldier to 'liberate' the younger members of a village community and suggests that the causes for his tragic failure lie in the persistence of age-old superstitions. Using the structure of the traditional melodrama, *Yellow Earth*, like the films that followed it, employed metaphor and a complex series of visual signifiers to convey its message.

Chapter 4 examines the beliefs and influence upon Chinese film and film-making as well as much else of China's foremost moral philosopher Confucius (551–479 BC). His belief that a harmonious society consisted of a strictly hierarchical system where each person knew his or her obligations and observed them through prescribed behaviour was enshrined in an examination system. This guaranteed the emperor a perpetual supply of bureaucrats to rule his vast territory. Although the first stirrings against Confucianism and its ills took place between 1916–20, Mao Zedong firmly identified Confucianism as an exploitative ideology and launched campaigns against it, whilst at the same time benefiting from the Chinese habits of compliance to impose his own brand of authority.

The status of women was perhaps the most profound change experienced under Mao. Formerly subject to enforced marriage, prostitution and slavery, women gained a measure of independence from new marriage and property laws. Enrolment in the job market and military activities, birth control and domestic support encouraged women to play a fuller part in wider society. At the same time male resistance and the failure of Communism to address feminist issues hampered the elimination of traditional practices. The representation of women in films reflected men's changing requirements of them, and the new wave films presented them for the first time as complex beings with legitimate sexual and social aims. They also reflected the general frustrations of a society demanding allegiance to political ends before sexual fulfilment. Whilst rebelling against the traditional roles they were still apparently presented as objects for the male cinemagoers' gaze. Unhappy marriages and children as a source of conflict remain the norm in Fifth Generation films. Zhang Yimou's film *Ju Dou* (1989) shows the vulnerability of women and the way in which traditional expectations of Confucian values operate against the interests of women in Chinese society.

Chapter 5 charts the changes in the structure of the Chinese economy after Mao's death and some aspects of the relationship between the Western powers and China. Following Mao's death in 1978, his successor Deng Xiaoping instituted a range of reforms in an attempt to kick-start an ailing economy. After the arrest and trials of the Gang of Four, Deng began to put into place mechanisms for the encouragement of private enterprise at home and foreign investment from abroad. This allowed consumerism to grow as incomes increased and the new information technology spread.

The economic reforms that were necessary to promote Deng's new vision of prosperity for China led to increased calls for democracy. Growing inequalities became evident as new freedoms to make private profits were exploited and the resulting inflation was felt particularly harshly by public sector workers. There was unrest in universities as students petitioned for better conditions and freedoms enjoyed by their Western counterparts. Population-control measures led to abuses and evasions that attracted the censure by Human Rights workers at the same time as Deng was seeking Western financial investment.

Two decades of demonstrations and clampdowns were characterised by inflation, housing shortages, growing materialism and financial corruption within the Party. Furthermore, rapid development of technology loosened government control of the spread of information and aided the growth of a dissident underground movement. In June 1989 these factors all came to a head when the government acted against hundreds of thousands of demonstrators in Tiananmen Square by sending in the People's Liberation Army to disperse them, using tanks and weapons. This chapter explores these issues in detail with reference to the cinematic production of the era.

Chapter 6 looks at how the political upheavals contributed to the rise of a new generation of film-makers. An underground movement gave rise to a so-called 'Sixth Generation' of film-makers whose aims and experiences were quite different from their predecessors. Concerned with the hardships of urban living for disaffected youths and intellectuals, they focused more narrowly on the personal lives of their protagonists and adopted documentary techniques suited to their resources and the need for secrecy. Meanwhile, a commercialised film industry encouraged a formulaic and conservative output that increasingly competed with Hollywood productions. Some of the foremost dissident directors, such as Zhang Yuan and Wang Xiaoshuai, have followed the example of Zhang Yimou in attempting to make films with seemingly contradictory qualities of questioning society whilst conforming to censorship requirements. They have become accepted into the closely censored studio-based system, albeit at some cost to integrity and authenticity.

This chapter considers Wang Xiaoshuai's *The Days* (1993) which depicts the daily tedium and lack of opportunity experienced by two artists working in a barracks-like setting in Beijing. After their visit to parents exiled to a remote region for political reasons, they experience the break-down of their relationship, caused by psychological pressures, and culminating in the young woman's escape to the West.

It is hoped that through the exploration of the social, political and economic contexts of Chinese cinema in the 1980s and 1990s, and the specific analysis of some of the most widely distributed and highly praised films to have emerged from China in recent decades, this book will aid in the understanding and appreciation of the many ways in which Chinese film-makers have sought to challenge official representations of cultural practice and so have in themselves presented challenging representations to the regime and the Chinese people. While in no way an exhaustive account, this introductory study is intended to inspire and promote further research into this important area of contemporary Film Studies, both in terms of debates surrounding 'national cinemas' and in illuminating a fascinating set of issues that touch on the nature and role of the moving image in a specific cultural and historical context.

1   SOME RECENT HISTORY

When Rius describes the story of Mao Zedong as 'the story of Modern China' (Rius & Friends 1980: 7) he is right in two senses. Mao's lifespan (1893–1976) encompassed the overthrow of the ancient dynastic system, the foundation of the Chinese Republic and the introduction of a system of government modelled on Marxism. He also made possible the modernisation of China.

Mao was aware at an early age of the poverty and inequality within Chinese society. Born on 26 December 1893 in Shaoshan, Hunan Province, He was the son of a landworker who had amassed a sizeable amount of land after years of poverty. In his talks with the American journalist Edgar Snow, Mao described the antagonisms in his immediate family and how he came to form a close alliance with his mother (Snow 1937). His later attempts to liberate women from feudal marriage customs probably originated from his observation of his mother's experience, whilst the troubled relationship with his father appears to have exacerbated his rebelliousness and taste for revolution.

At the age of 14 Mao refused an arranged marriage to a Miss Luo whom his father moved into the household, eventually leaving to study in a nearby town. Here, his hero was a teacher who had cut off his pigtail in defiance of the demands of the Manchu rulers but wore a false one to keep his position. When he was 16 he enrolled at Xinjiang Institute and studied Chinese History.

In Mao's childhood, over 90 per cent of people lived in the countryside, for the most part eking out a precarious existence and subject to
frequent natural disasters with no welfare provision. In 1887–88 a famine
in northern China killed up to 10 million people through starvation and
left many more displaced. A growing population meant less to eat and
over half of the land was owned by 10 per cent of the population, who on
the whole treated peasants badly. They were also taxed by unscrupulous
local officials acting on behalf of the Emperor.

In addition to oppressive rulers, China was also subject to foreign
invaders. Foreign occupation partly resulted from treaties signed when
Chinese resistance to the opium trade was overcome by the British,
anxious to redress the imbalance of debt incurred through the export of
tea and silk. Their rights to occupy and to trade were extended to other
nations. Missionaries adopted a diplomatic silence and by 1858, when the
Manchu rulers of the Qing dynasty were forced to make further conces-
sions, a significant number of Europeans and Americans were living in
Beijing. By the start of the twentieth century, almost all of China's foreign
trade and ports were controlled by foreigners, as well as the railways,
commerce, banking and the silk industry. Foreigners treated the Chinese
much as the landowners treated the peasants and the apocryphal story is
told of Mao visiting Shanghai as a young man and noticing a sign at the
entrance to the main park that read 'No admittance to Chinese or dogs'.

In 1911, the Qing dynasty was overthrown. Mao had moved to a larger
school in the provincial capital, Changsha, where he joined a rebel army
under the leadership of Sun Yat-sen, a revolutionary leader who founded
Republican China in 1912. By 1918 Mao was working in Beijing at the
University where he encountered such prejudice from academics that it
gave rise to a lifelong dislike of the intellectual elite.

Mao returned to Changsha in 1919 to teach at a primary school and
wrote articles in favour of women's rights for a new journal and organised protests against Japan, which had been given control of German
possessions on Chinese soil after the end of World War One. In 1920 he
married Yang Kaihui, the daughter of a Beijing professor, and they had
two sons. He initiated a secret Communist Party cell and, in keeping with

traditional Marxism, called for revolution to be led by urban workers, although he increasingly perceived a conflict between official Marxist theory and China's conditions.

After 1916 China was a country of warlords with a capitalist economy but no central government with any real political power. Sun Yat-sen had reorganised the Guomindang nationalist army but had little success against the warlords and in 1923 Lenin offered Sun financial backing provided he would accept Chinese Communists into the ranks. However, this lasted only until 1927. Mao felt frustrated because middle-class intellectuals ignored his urgings for members to think about the peasants and so went back to Hunan to organise peasants to take land from the wealthy, despite Party opposition. In 1925, following the death of Sun Yat-sen, Chiang Kai-shek assumed control of the Guomindang. At first he allied with the Communists to overthrow the warlords who had taken over parts of China, but Mao offended Chiang by predicting that peasants would take over, and in April 1927 Chiang sent troops to Shanghai to track down Communists and attack striking workers. Thousands were killed in the battles that followed. Mao was to lead an uprising in Hunan, which proved to be a failure. Convinced more than ever that the power of the peasants was the correct force to harness, Mao escaped with troops to a mountainous region between Hunan and Jianxi provinces.

Mao's wife stayed in Changsha, and Mao embarked on an affair with a young Communist League member called He Zizhen. A few years later his first wife and sister were to be tortured and killed by the Guomindang because of their relationship to Mao. By 1934 Mao had three million people and thousands of square miles under his control. On 16 October he began the greatest military march in history – The Long March. His so-called Red Army and a few thousand civilians, including He Zizhen, fought their way through the encircling Guomindang. The two children they left behind were never found again. 120,000 people began the Long March but fewer than 10,000 finished it. Along the way the Red Army preached revolution, redistributed land and demonstrated Communism's ideals.

A year later Mao and the survivors arrived at an enclave in Shaanxi, 6,000 miles from where they had begun. Mao was a charismatic leader and brilliant strategist; the Long March from Kiangsi to Yan'an made him a hero. The relationship with He Zizhen ended after they arrived in Yan'an and he married a former actress, later to become known as the infamous Jiang Qing, leader of the Gang of Four. Their stormy relationship produced one daughter. In all, Mao fathered nine children, of whom only four survived to adulthood.

In 1932 the Japanese had invaded Manchurian northern China and by 1938 occupied all the major population centres. Mao agreed a truce with Chiang Kai-shek to drive out the Japanese, who were defeated in 1945, not by Mao but by the United States and the Western Allies. In 1949 Mao's army, now officially known as the People's Liberation Army, finally overcame Chiang's nationalist Guomindang army, which fled to Taiwan.

Mao's achievements

Mao was 56 years old and faced with a ruined country: industry, agriculture and trade devastated, almost total illiteracy, rampant disease, misery, hunger, and high unemployment. The sole available model of a country that had become relatively advanced without the involvement of capitalists was Soviet Russia. Stalin aided Mao with Soviet technicians, technology, an education programme and a loan of $300 million. Facing disarray in the cities, Mao adopted the Soviet model for expediency. Inflation was controlled, industry nationalised and planned, and students were trained in sciences, mainly in Russia. New schools opened and factories were built.

In 1957 Mao turned away from the Soviet model of development: relations with Soviet leader Krushchev were strained because Stalin, whom Krushchev had condemned, was much admired in China. A mass movement swept China in 1958: in communes ranging in size up to 20,000 strong, peasants would pool resources to support locally needed industries. Communes were to set up schools and small technical institutes as the first step to combine modern science and traditional agricultural wisdom. Rudimentary health clinics were set up as well as communal laundries and grain mills, and there was an increase in electrification and new water projects. On 2 May 1956 Mao launched 'The Hundred Flowers Movement'. The policy, based on an ancient saying, was to 'Let a hundred flowers blossom, a hundred schools of thought contend' and was meant to cover all areas of endeavour, including literature and the arts. However, Mao was not prepared for the barrage of complaints that followed: on 8 June 1957 an anti-rightist backlash followed and many artists were punished. Mao then announced the Great Leap Forward, to be implemented from December 1957. Industrial development was at the heart of the policy, which led to the development of 'backyard furnaces'. Although this failed to produce steel of usable quality, there was a growth of other small-scale industries and the development of coal mines in rural areas. Owing to vast manpower resources the area of irrigated land in China doubled in six months, and production in all sectors of the economy increased substantially (see David 1993).

The number of communes increased, with the aim of breaking the ties of Confucianism and laying the foundations of collective life. Mao also saw a need to transform peasants into wage-earners so they would become 'agricultural workers' with land held collectively. He instigated the organisation of civilians into militia to reinforce China's military strength. Some liberation of women from domestic duties was achieved through the establishment of nurseries and communal canteens so they could play a full part in the work force. The commune was to be responsible for all aspects of life, including health and social welfare. Long work hours were followed by study classes in socialist ideology.

The Great Leap Forward ended in economic failure owing to natural disasters and widespread crop failures, compounded by industrial management problems, flood damage and drought. Between 1959 and 1962 divisions amongst China's leaders were increasingly apparent, and Mao was criticised by Chinese and Russians alike. Liu Shaoqi took over the leadership from Mao, who retired from day-to-day politics, with Deng Xiaoping becoming Secretary General of the Party. In the early 1960s the policies of the government under Liu encouraged the growth of capitalism on a small scale. Although economic stability began to be restored it was in contradiction to Mao's socialist goals, and despite the welfare of the masses being somewhat sacrificed, a measure of economic stability was achieved under the leadership of Liu Shaoqi.

Mao perceived that the Communist Party in China was riddled with those wanting to promote the interests of their own families, and stated that even the Ministry of Health served only an elite section of urban society. Women's positions were still largely unchanged whilst intellectuals had none of the revolutionary vision of young people and only wanted to make money from their knowledge. Encouraged by Mao, who held mass rallies and addressed crowds of his youthful Red Army volunteers, millions of young people were mobilised to attack authority figures and destroy the symbols of privilege in a great 'Cultural Revolution'. In the ensuing abandonment of formal learning and attacks on academics, the universities were closed for nearly four years, and President Liu Shaoqi was arrested.

Mao became a national cult figure; no-one dared speak against him for fear of being attacked as a 'rightist'. His closest ally and most outspoken advocate, Lin Biao, compiled a collection of Mao's writings in 1964 that became known as the Little Red Book. However, Lin Biao died in a mysterious plane-crash in 1971, after a rumoured abortive attempt to seize power.

In July 1966, at the age of 72, Mao swam nine miles down the Yangtse River indicating he was still in vigorous health. This was a temporary situation, though, and as his health began to fail, new leaders emerged, including Mao's wife Jiang Qing. Her closest allies were Zhang Chunqiao, Wang Hongwen and Yao Wenyuan, afterwards to become notorious as the Gang of Four. Extremists, they were convinced that it had been a mistake in the 1950s to allow the old cultural traditions to continue and they zealously attacked writers, dancers, scholars and the Beijing Opera.

Newspapers were full of articles exhorting the people to further action against groups perceived as reactionaries in influential areas such as education. Thought-reform meetings were held weekly so people could be told the correct way of thinking; critics were sent to labour camps and a climate of fear prevailed. In April 1976 the Gang of Four provoked rioting in Beijing and other cities by their refusal to allow the commemoration of popular leader Zhou Enlai at the Qing Ming Festival, when the Chinese traditionally honour the dead. Mao died on 9 September 1976, aged 83, having nominated his successor, Hua Guofeng. Hua immediately overthrew the Gang of Four, a decision that was to prove very popular, and a new era of change began.

Opening doors

After Mao's death, those he had called 'capitalist-roaders' – people who believed in co-operating with Western powers – were reinstated. Mao was replaced by Deng Xiaoping, who had twice been purged for his rightist views, although at first he was deputy to Mao's nominated successor, Hua Guofeng. The excesses of the Cultural Revolution had discredited Mao's policies, however, and it was not to Hua Guofeng's advantage that he was Mao's chosen successor: he resigned in June 1981, not long before the Central Committee testified to Mao's greatness whilst censuring his actions since 1957. Although Mao had made mistakes, 'Mao Zedong Thought' – his special brand of interpreting Communism – continued to be reinforced, although his personality cult and over-zealous pursuit of revolution were condemned.

The Gang of Four, who had enforced 'red over expert' policies, were blamed for the violent excesses of the Cultural Revolution, arrested within four weeks of Mao's death and prosecuted in 1980–81 in a highly publicised set of trials. During the ten years of revolution ordinary people had been persecuted for having bourgeois ancestry or any contact with the West and many did not survive; around 17 million youths had been sent to the countryside, and thousands died as a result. The Gang of Four were held ultimately responsible for around 35,000 deaths, at a conservative estimate.

Deng Xiaoping had long revolutionary credentials: he was active with Zhou Enlai in France in the 1920s, worked in the Shanghai underground movement, was a Long March veteran, and had practised guerrilla warfare against Japan. He was General Secretary of the Communist Party in 1956 and had twice been ousted from power during the Cultural Revolution.

Deng thought some of Mao's campaigns, such as the Hundred Flowers movement, the Great Leap Forward and the Anti-Rightist movements were too extreme, but 'dismantled Maoism without discrediting Mao' (David 1993: 300). He believed people would work harder for material incentives so set up bonus and enterprise schemes in industry and agriculture, gave state concerns more autonomy and instigated a free market economy. Deng also set up programmes for students to study science and technology abroad. Since taking power in 1978, he put increased emphasis on raising incomes, saying that socialism did not mean poverty. Ideology and class struggle faded into the background and Deng formulated the Four Modernisations (of agriculture, industry, technology, and defence) along with the Four Cardinal Principles (retaining the socialist path, the dictatorship of the proletariat, the leadership of the Communist Party, and the ideology of Marxism, Leninism and Maoism).

In 1979 he introduced the idea of Special Economic Zones where facilities were offered to foreigners to build plants and employ locals. Investors were given tax breaks and other financial incentives such as the development of a transport infrastructure. In direct contradiction to Mao's self-sufficiency policies he began courting foreign investors, encouraging joint ventures between foreign firms and Chinese government agencies. Foreign manufacturers were attracted by low labour costs and the market for goods such as vehicles; they also manufactured goods for the Western market. Guandong province, with access to Hong Kong, did particularly well. The fastest way to modernise was to import foreign technology and most planners abandoned Mao's proscriptions in the rush to obtain foreign currency.

Deng's policies led to the tripling of average incomes by the early 1990s, moving, according to World Bank calculations, 170 million peasants out of poverty. In 1978 the dismantling of collective agriculture began and the Agricultural Responsibility System was instigated, where rural households were assigned land they could treat as their own and were given incentives to increase production. Sideline activities such as pig farming and other small business concerns were encouraged. In coastal areas, where opportunities for commercial enterprises were greatest, incomes increased most, and eased restrictions on movement meant people could move to where the jobs were and send money home.

The Responsibility System, adopted by over 90 per cent of peasant families, led to increased production and more buying power for the peasants, stimulating demand for consumer articles such as television sets and washing and sewing machines. With the development of rural industry and the building of small towns it was predicted that 70 per cent of the population would be out of agriculture by the year 2000. Family workshops grew in number, producing a variety of small articles from electric push-buttons to hair-pins, encouraged by capital investment by the State.

Furthermore, there were considerable improvements in health care and education in China. University education remained free and a number of technical and vocational institutes were set up all over the country. Some universities organised exchange relationships with universities in other countries and many foreign specialists and scholars accepted the invitation to teach in China. The emphasis on education was that it should respond to the needs of the economy, and bonuses and attractive living conditions were established to support teachers. Deng also pushed for the better education of Party officials: in the early 1980s only four per cent of the 40 million or so Party members had a college education. College entrance examinations were reinstituted in 1977 and students motivated by a desire to study abroad started a widespread interest in learning English.

There was also a revival of literature after 1978 with an emphasis on realism in modern works, and over 400 literary magazines now publish novels, stories, poems and essays. Theatre arts flourish, as do orchestras and choirs and the practice of arts and crafts has been greatly revived. Media has proliferated, including newspapers, television and radio, with signs of a more liberal attitude towards content. In 1988 a popular six-part television drama called 'River Elegy' attacked Chinese inward-looking tendencies and blamed backwardness on the stagnation of old philosophies. In October 1987, for the thirteenth congress of the CCP, Western reporters were allowed in for the first time.

Film and persuasion

The CCP made early moves in 1949 to bring the film industry under their control. The chief barrier to communicating their ideals was the persistence of traditional ideas and behaviours in a vast territory where 80 per cent of the population work on the land and where Confucian ethics continue to heavily influence attitudes.

Film was soon recognised by the Party leaders as a very powerful means of persuasion in a situation where they needed to impress on the people a model of behaviour and a belief system that were in many ways contradictory to established traditions and customs. Some aspects of these, such as the structure of the family and the power of the father to choose husbands for his daughters, were particularly intractable and bound up with quasi-religious practices, notably Confucianism with its emphasis on hierarchical family and social obligations. The government's most powerful argument was to link their ideology with the idea of nationhood and appeal to an ingrained sense of patriotism or the uniqueness of what it meant to be Chinese. This was particularly important at a time when restoration of a sense of national autonomy was in progress, especially in relation to the position of foreigners. The Soviet Union provided a model of socialism that could be adopted for reasons of expediency, and Russians, although foreigners, were untainted by a connection with Japanese or other European invaders who had occupied parts of China in the past.

Film can, when it examines the state of the nation, call into question the whole idea of nationhood and deconstruct the idea of the nation as a unified entity. Such representations, like other ideological constructions, are the sites of considerable competition: 'To gain control of the representational agenda for the nation is to gain considerable power over the individuals view of themselves and each other' (Turner 1988: 13). The satellite countries, Hong Kong, Singapore and Taiwan, of course, compete in providing such alternative ideologies.

If the persuasive power of film could be harnessed to government aims, it was also a source of potential social disruption. Film critic Bin

Zhao remarks on the absence of an investigative social science in China between 1919 and 1989 and says that 'it was left to the arts to play a key role in providing social criticism' (Bin 1994: 34). Coupled with a concern to control representation at home was a growing awareness of the need for a positive image abroad, although this was less important in the early days. When viewed in the West, films set in China constitute a major source of cultural information, what Chow describes as 'a front' and 'an arcade in the international culture marketplace' (Chow 1995: 26). In the 1980s this was an increasingly important concern of the Chinese government, who did not want their country to be represented as a backward nation of superstition-ridden peasants.

The government thus needed to present itself in a positive light to its own people: in attempting to industrialise and modernise society they were also trying to avoid the mistakes and consequences of rapid industrialisation as experienced in the West, particularly in regard to the overpopulation of towns and the breakdown of the extended family unit. Instead of the perceived individualistic greed for material advancement, Mao and his allies wanted to establish a society based on collaborative effort and socialist ideals and so needed to mobilise support for change on a massive scale whilst avoiding negative messages about themselves and their right to govern. A recurring message of films made during the period 1949–66 was therefore the need to sacrifice individual gain for the sake of the nation.

A typical story of self-abnegation in the service of the state is shown in *The Girls from Shanghai* (1958), about two youngsters who meet whilst working on a construction project. Although the young man at first harbours personal ambitions and is full of ill-thought-out schemes, he accepts the guidance of his more down-to-earth companions and low-key romance flourishes as they share a mutual idealism which inspires their efforts. The setting and characters are typical of films under Mao, the protagonists workers rather than intellectuals, engaged in manual labour, minimising or completely obliterating any suggestion of sexual attraction. Such films contrast with those made in the West at this time, where a boy-girl relationship was synonymous with sexual attraction. Hollywood released *The Tunnel of Love* in the same year, in which an expensively dressed Doris Day, offered, as usual, sexual favours in return for marriage, in this case to Gig Young. Boy-girl relationships as viewed as skirmish was echoed in the explicit title of *The Mating Game* (1958), starring Debbie Reynolds and Tony Randall, whilst the teenage protagonists of *High School Confidential*, another 1958 release, inhabited a sleazy world of sex and drugs. In the same year *Cat on a Hot Tin Roof*, starring Elizabeth Taylor and Paul Newman, concentrated on the sexual problems of the wealthy protagonists, ignoring the political issues of the American South, which formed a folksy backdrop to the personal dramas.

A further argument for the control of representation in the modern world is that people are increasingly aware of themselves as actors in the field of public events. Mao's dramatic personal appearances at Tiananmen Square, like those of Hitler at the Nuremberg rallies, could be described, as Chow argues, as a 'filmic' event for Chinese youths, who 'entered awareness of themselves as "interpellated", not as watchers of film, but as film itself' (Chow 1995: 10). In the Tiananmen Square dramas of 1989, the figure of the lone protester facing the tanks, flashed onto television screens on a global scale, became a powerful world-wide image of Chinese government oppression. In its early stages, when television access was restricted, film was the most important media for presenting images of themselves to the people.

The 'socialist family' ideal was promoted in films such as *Revolutionary Family* (1961) in which a mother sacrifices the life of her son rather than reveal the identities of underground revolutionaries to her Nationalist tormentors.

Lastly, cinema presents a portrait of life as lived by 'ordinary' people. Traditionally, true 'Chineseness' has been associated through literary representation with Confucian ideas of 'the gentleman' – a privileged member of the Mandarin class who gained admission to powerful positions through wealth and a bureaucratic examination system. But the 'democratising' effect of film radically changed this and allowed the majority to identify more easily with the people represented. *Dragon's Beard Ditch* (1952) about residents banding together to improve the local environment, and *Our Niu Baisui* (1984), about different reactions of farmers to the rural reform of the late 1970s, showed how people helped build the new China. The concerns of ordinary Chinese people became the focus of narrative entertainment, more traditionally associated with the rich and powerful. Cinema was thus very significantly made to seem more relevant to ordinary lives.

Film since 1949

The history of Chinese film since the founding of the People's Republic in 1949 is usually divided into three periods: the 17 years from the take-over of the Communist Party in 1949 up to the outbreak of the Cultural Revolution in 1966, the Cultural Revolution years until 1976, and the 'Modern Era', from then to the present.

The Chinese Film Industry was somewhat uneven in its early development, for demographic and financial reasons. Audiences tended to be concentrated in Shanghai and the other treaty ports, with a largely separate development in Hong Kong. By the late 1930s and 1940s, films with a high standard of technical and artistic quality were being produced by private as well as government-controlled studios. A very early example was *Spring Silkworm* (1933) about threats to the livelihoods of silk producers near Shanghai by greedy landlords and foreign imports and *A Spring River Flows East* (1947), an epic two-part film about a family during the time of the war of resistance against Japan.

These celebrated films were in the humanist-socialist tradition that followed in the wake of the so-called 'May Fourth' liberal intellectual movement, begun in 1919. An attempt to modernise and revitalise China, it was launched as a protest against the Treaty of Versailles, which gave Japan the Shandong Province and went on to become a long-lived cultural reform movement. The films concerned the lives and preoccupations of mainly urban households and were critical of social conditions. The studios enjoyed considerable freedom to produce films for their audience and even felt able to ignore direct government recommendations. This changed when the CCP took control.

After the 1949 victory of the People's Liberation Army (PLA) the industry was still recovering from shortages of film stock and resources caused by almost 40 years of civil war, but there was no shortage of trained personnel. Several documentaries, in addition to newsreels, had been made at the Communist base at Yan'an during the Civil War years. The very first feature film produced by the People's Republic of China was *The Bridge* in April 1949, the plot centring on workers' enthusiasm for a building project. After the film industry was nationalised, the appearance in November of that same year of *Daughters of China*, an ambitious nationalistic saga, was an indication of the new haste to make films. Both films were produced by the China Film Studio, equipped with materials liberated from the former Japanese studio in Manchuria. The Beijing Film Studio was also established in 1949, as was the Shanghai Film Studio, the latter being the best equipped, with the largest film-making capacity.

Cinema at this time was still catering mainly to largely city-based audiences but the Party's aim was to secure a larger national audience and by this means expand the process of political education, to teach new values and ideas. Mao Zedong's 'Talks at the Yan'an forum on Literature and Art', and the Literary Rectification campaign of the same year, changed perceptions of the aims of writers and artists in China: the role of art was primarily to contribute to educating the people about Communist ideals. Thereafter a number of policies were implemented, with campaigns and purges to suppress dissenting film-makers. Films produced between 1949 and 1966, including some 800 feature films, fully reflected the Party's agenda.

The CCP had already recognised the importance of film as a propaganda weapon. As early as 1932 an underground Communist cell in Shanghai had been formed with the intention of infiltrating the film industry. During the war of resistance against the Japanese occupation, many Communist intellectuals worked in the propaganda department of the coalition government under Chiang Kai-shek. The Central Film Bureau was set up to take charge of the entire industry.

There was a spate of production of 'socialist reconstruction' films, such as *Sisters Stand Up* (1951), in which government work to stamp out prostitution was praised, and *City Without Night* (1957), about the transformation of Shanghai capitalists during the campaign to nationalise private industries. Credible characterisation and likely outcomes were disregarded and messages about moral reform and regeneration took precedence. Many were based on already-popular film forms such as war films, musicals, or, as in *City Without Night*, Shanghai decadence films.

As well as introducing the kind of films that propagated Party values they also began to purge Western films, especially Hollywood products. This was done by limiting the number of days they could be shown and sponsoring campaigns against them. There was some social stigma attached to watching US films after the government mounted demonstrations against them, so that by 1950 American films were almost non-existent in China. The gap was filled with films from the Soviet Union and Eastern Europe; between 1949 and 1952 a total of 180 Soviet films were dubbed. Ticket prices were lowered in towns and the news media were employed to help Chinese audiences understand the unfamiliar cultural background to the films. Chinese film-makers were sent to the Soviet Union for training and Russian film-makers invited to teach in the Beijing Film School, later renamed the Beijing Film Academy.

In 1950 the government developed a quota system to keep studios to an annual production plan and allocated the subject matter of films appropriate to the Party's concerns at the time. Following Mao's Yan'an injunctions, the mood of home-produced films was to be celebratory, with a stress on victory against the enemy, whether Guomindang, Japanese invaders or American imperialists. The emphasis was to be on struggle, resulting in the triumph of good over evil. There was rapid development in the production of film scripts during this period, with discussions and instructive seminars on film theory led by the Russians. After 1949 there was no other suitable model to learn from than Soviet cinema, which had already achieved some films of remarkable quality in the socialist-realist mode. After the visits of Soviet film experts in 1953, film production and administration methods were all based on the Soviet system. This had its drawbacks, however, as film schools were set up lacking staff and materials.

Films subscribing to the idea of 'socialist realism' began to be produced, showing 'positive heroes primarily interested in the betterment of the masses, class struggle, the eventual triumph of the progressive forces over reactionary forces' (Tam & Dissanayake 1998: 3–4). *Dong Cunrui* (1955), about a soldier who gives his life to save his comrades, was presented as a model for Communist youths to follow, and was among a number of popular war films made to the prescribed pattern. *Capture Mount Hua by Stratagem* (1953) was about a Communist command force overtaking a strategically important nationalist stronghold. Advance troops from a Communist brigade enlist the help of a herb-gathering pharmacist who reveals the secret pathways up the mountain to the enemy stronghold. With further help from a Nationalist deserter they take control of the area and eliminate all enemy resistance.

Film imports from other countries were banned during this period, whilst historical sagas appealed by virtue of lavish production values and attention to historical details, such as *The Opium War* (1959) about efforts to control Opium imports from Britain in the mid-nineteenth century and in which the protests of the masses contrast with the selfish attitude of the ruling Qin Emperor. Another popular film was *The First Sino-Japanese War* (1962), a story of heroic resistance to the Japanese in the late nineteenth century.

By the early 1960s film-makers trained with Soviet help were producing good quality films such as *Serfs* (1964), depicting male and female Tibetan land-slaves rescued by the PLA, one of many films which depicted the gratitude of minority peoples saved from feudal systems, including *Li Shuangshuang* (1962) which focuses upon a woman commune leader who reforms her own husband, and *Third Sister Liu* (1960), a musical about a Tang Dynasty peasant girl who stands up to despotic landlords. Films like this last one aimed to show minority people participating in class struggle.

When the CCP first took greater control of the film industry, the government sought to encourage private studios awarding loans and providing film stock and equipment. All this changed when the private studios were judged to be producing films contrary to government policy. Campaigns were mounted against many of them, the most famous of which was *The Life of Wu Xun* (1950), based on the real-life story of a peasant. This was attacked by Mao, and all involved in its making were subject to public pressure and many were forced to recant in public or offer written 'self-criticisms'. Government disapproval meant poor box-office, and this had a discouraging effect on the entire industry. Rates of production dropped, studios began to merge, and film-makers were preoccupied with not making mistakes. In 1952 the last of the private studios merged with Shanghai Film Studio and were to remain non-existent for the next three decades.

The government's ambitious programme of films was cut short with the outbreak of the Korean War in 1950. After 29 projects were realised in 1950, only five further features had been made by 1953. After that, production steadily increased, with 13 features in 1953, 24 in 1955 and 42 in 1956, when the Hundred Flowers campaign seemed to offer new cultural freedom. There was an effort to establish studios outside the main film cities in 1957, particularly in the autonomous regions such as Mongolia. New studios made the most of their films as co-productions with major studios, a pattern continued until the Cultural Revolution.

With the launch of the Hundred Flowers movement in May 1956, audiences were treated for a short time to a cinema that once again turned its attention to human concerns and the pre-liberation subjects of feelings and actions, as opposed to state propaganda. An anti-rightist backlash followed the welter of complaints in response to Mao's apparent invitation to comment on social problems. Zhang Dianfei, a much-respected film critic, was labelled a rightist and there were other attacks on film artists and films that presented a perceived deviation from socialist principles. Zhou Enlai, noting the drop in quality after the tide of purges, suggested an emphasis on documentary, so there were many such 'educational' films made in 1958.

As with all areas of Chinese life, the Great Leap Forward overturned the film industry. Studios were established in 19 provinces and three municipalities, as well as four of five autonomous regions (the exception being Tibet), each under the direct control of central government. The 'Leap' was in quantity only, with studios continuing to produce mainly documentary-style art films and filmed state operas. Notable examples, all from 1958, are *Bells Ring in Green Valley*, about heroic efforts to achieve and surpass grain targets; *A Thousand Miles a Day*, three stories about successes in agriculture and industry during the Great Leap; and *Young Masters of the Great Leap Forward*, in which young people in various sectors make their contribution.

In an effort to rectify poor quality in 1959, Zhou suggested good films could be made for the People's Republic of China's fortieth anniversary. This inspired some better quality films such as *The Lin Family Shop* (1959) about how profiteering among businessmen harms ordinary people, described as 'a graphic exposition of how the CCP viewed the national bourgeoisie' (Zhang & Xiao 1998: 225), and *Five Golden Flowers* (1959), a musical comedy in which a Spring festival romance between a young man and a commune leader he searches for shows ethnic minority solidarity in the effort for the Great Leap.

In 1960, following Mao's break with the Soviet model of development, Russian trainers and aid were abruptly withdrawn and China was left with a shortage of funds and trained expertise. China terminated nearly all cultural exchanges with foreigners, and in the early 1960s film-makers concentrated on turning out films to reflect cultural traditions and national characteristics. Some good examples are 1961's *The Red Detachment of Women*, where a former slave becomes a revolutionary fighter; *Early Spring in February* (1963), in which a well-meaning young school teacher's devotion to helping others leads to his becoming a revolutionary; and *Stage Sisters* (1965), a story of actress friends divided by politics until they are united to serve a revolutionary opera troupe.

During the Cultural Revolution the industry was much affected by malevolent political forces, led by Lin Biao and Jiang Qing, which very nearly destroyed the film industry entirely. Although 47 features had been made in 1965, only four were made in 1966 before the Cultural Revolution brought production to a halt. The China Film Archive closed, the three film schools stopped teaching, and almost all existing films were withdrawn from circulation. Limited production began again in 1970 but this 'gave the industry that had employed over 60,000 people in 1959 nothing to do but transfer "model revolutionary works" from one medium to another' (Rayns & Meek 1980: 7).

The Western gaze

Since the early years of the twentieth century, screenings of Western films in China, with their negative portrayals of Chinese culture and people, provoked protests from the Chinese. These representations were generally dictated by the political climate of the time. The most negative portrayals were seen in the British series of Fu Man Chu films dated between the 1920s and the 1940s. Invented by writer Sax Rohmer, a London-based journalist, in a series of short stories published in 1912, Dr Fu Man Chu was an evil arch-villain who enjoyed almost supernatural powers through ancient knowledge, and an opium addict. Fu was the leader of a secret group dedicated to ruling the world, and 'the embodiment of a white racist's nightmare' (Hawley 1991: 135).

The films are full of blatant colonial imagery – evil Orientals form a contrasting backdrop for a white upper-class hero, Sir Denis Nayland, 'a figure of Western acumen pitted against Eastern cunning' (Clegg 1994: 1). One of the best known was *The Yellow Claw* (1920) which concerned drug trafficking and portrayed the Chinese underworld of London's East End. The film's most memorable iconography was a yellow claw that appeared mysteriously through gaps in walls. Another film that also dealt with the perceived drug threat was *Cocaine* (1922), advertised by a poster showing a leering Chinese. It attracted large audiences and provoked a protest to the Home Office from the Chinese community.

In America, China had long been considered 'inscrutable', mostly because of the restricted flow of information, and so people were much more than usually dependent on 'the kaleidoscope of images available in fiction and film' (Hawley 1991: 132). The desire for information was such that between 1920 and 1940 *The Saturday Evening Post*, the most popular and widely-read American magazine at the time, published a story with an Asian cast or setting every other month. In the 1920s the protagonist of any Chinese story was likely to be a variation on the 'diabol-ical' Chinaman.

American films contained a range of Chinese stereotypes. Most preva-lent was the evil Mandarin – a well-to-do Chinese with mysterious powers who appeared in a number of films such as *Broken Fetters* (1916), *The Yellow Menace* (1916), and *Mr Wu* (1920). Less sinister was the Chinese pirate or bandit who was mainly seen chasing goods or money but who also showed an interest in white women. He appeared in *Shanghai Bound* (1927), *Tell it to the Marines* (1927), and *China Seas* (1935). The Chinese equivalent of the American gangster, the warlord, appeared in American films in the late 1920s and 1930s. He resembled a military variation of the evil mandarin, and combined a disregard for human life with a taste for torture. His prototype was General Yang in *The General Died at Dawn* (1936). A variation was General Yen in *The Bitter Tea of General Yen* (1932) who, although despotic, was portrayed as the hero of the film in a story of romance between a Chinese warlord and an American missionary. In such films, any problems with miscegenation were normally resolved when the Chinese character turned out not to be Chinese, or when one of the lovers died. In the case of *The Bitter Tea of General Yen*, the Chinese General commits suicide by drinking poison.

The foremost of Chinese heroes was the detective. He was polite, gracious and well-mannered with a sense of humour, and he called on the wisdom of the past to apply to the present. The most famous was Charlie Chan. There were 48 Charlie Chan films, with six different main actors, none of whom was Chinese. In any case it was standard practice to have Chinese film characters played by Japanese, or even European, actors.

Portrayals of Chinese domestics such as house boys, cooks and laundry men date back to the 1920s and were often suspects in murder mysteries, although seldom found guilty. Their 'pidgin' English and long queues, or pig-tails, were often objects of ridicule and they were shown beaming foolishly as they completely misunderstood what was said to them. They were eliminated on purpose from films made before and during World War Two as offensive to the Chinese, and have not reappeared. The first positive portrayal of the Chinese on their native soil was that of the

Chinese peasant. In *The Good Earth* (1936), adapted from Pearl Buck's novel of the same name, he was shown to be hard-working, strong, persevering, respectful to elders and fond of children.

It was not until the 1930s and 1940s that the Chinese government took an active interest in the representation of the Chinese people in Hollywood films. This was due to the problems of internal conflict, famines and floods, in addition to the lack of any coherent sense of nationalism that would normally have aroused feelings of contempt for the way a nation was being represented on the international stage. In the early days of Hollywood there were few protests at unfavourable portrayals. But when, by the 1930s, there was the beginning of a functioning foreign service the Chinese began to object to negative representations. Protest from newly self-conscious nationalists took several forms, such as the refusal to distribute films with negative portrayals, or by making cuts. Official representatives began to approach studios and pressure was brought to bear to stop the distribution of offensive films outside the US. They asked world-wide diplomats to protest screenings. The US Foreign Trade Commission assisted by advising companies about the reasons for Chinese objections to certain types of material that had appeared in films. The studios themselves carried out self-censorship and shelved several 'warlord' projects. The studios also asked for advice concerning the appointment of technical advisors with a Chinese background to be assigned to films.

The earliest films about China shown in America were newsreels or documentaries made between 1898 and 1905. The first narrative film about China was a serial film with an Oriental villain. D. W. Griffith's *Broken Blossoms* (1919) was most the important film of this period, based on Thomas Burke's book 'Limehouse Nights', and in particular a story called 'The Chink and the Child'. The film had a sympathetic Chinese hero and started a string of films with Chinatown settings. They contrasted the sensitivity of the Chinese with a brutal English villain. Later films utilised Limehouse or the Chinatowns of large American cities for stories of crime and mystery set in China. The genre is found as late as the mid-1930s in *Limehouse Blues* (1934), starring George Raft and Anna Mae Wong.

Towards the end of the 1920s films began to be centred on gang warfare, gambling and smuggling. 1930s films were often based on documentaries, but contained large amounts of fantasy elements. Joseph von Sternberg's *The Shanghai Gesture* (1942) portrayed China in this earlier tradition but, in the main, war years' films were more realistic.

In the 1940s the new realistic portraits were clearly established in films such as *China Fights Back* (1941), clarifying China's battle against the Japanese. Feature films such as *Burma Convoy* (1941) and *A Yank on the Burma Road* (1942) attempted to show realistic portrayals of Chinese during the war. The most often repeated theme, however, was resistance to Japanese invaders, as in *Dragon Seed* (1944), again based on a Pearl Buck novel. The smuggling genre was also popular in the 1940s, however, reinforcing a connection between China and crime. There were some 'missionary' films, of which the best-known is *The Keys of the Kingdom* (1944), one of the top box office films of 1944–45.

American empathy with the Chinese resulted from Japanese attacks on China, which coincided with the release of *The Good Earth*. The later 1932 Shanghai fighting struck a chord of sympathy with the American public, and the incident known as The Rape of Nanking in December 1937, when the Japanese committed mass rape and the massacre of civilians, further enlisted American sympathy. The attack on Pearl Harbour in 1941 cemented for Americans positive impressions of the Chinese as victims of colonial aggressors, and a number of documentaries during World War Two fuelled American ideas of China as a land of 'heroic glamour' (Isaacs 1972: 174).

During the war, the Office of Information encouraged a favourable representation of China and issued a Government Information Manual on 6 June 1942. A film in which great efforts were made to ensure accuracy of portrayal was *The Keys of the Kingdom* (1944), the story of a Catholic missionary in the last years of the Manchu dynasty. Although initially unpopular with the Chinese, when finished it was well-reviewed and had only a few cuts before being released in China and other eastern countries. Positive portrayals of Orientals were more frequent during 1948, with eleven prominent roles given sympathetic characterisation. These became less favourable after the start of the Korean War and in 1953, for the first time, not one Oriental was portrayed in a sympathetic light.

No US films were made about China during the Mao years, but in films where Chinese characters do appear they are portrayed as evil 'reds'. *Hell and High Water* (1954) has a plot about a Communist plan to drop an atomic bomb on Korea or Manchuria and blame it on the US. In recent years, the Chinese are often portrayed as a close and conspiratorial group, masterminded by international Triad gangs. Chinese characters are regularly used to point up the superiority of white characters. Films such as Michael Cimino's *Year of the Dragon* (1985) and Abel Ferrara's *China Girl* (1987), set in New York's Chinatown, were particularly offensive in their representation of the Chinese. Media images today display 'a mixture of dramatic fight scenes, and pseudo-Eastern mysticism which play upon popular notions of the mysterious powers of the exotic East' (Clegg 1994: 37). The general pool of images of the Chinese in the West has been recently modified, however, by ironic portrayals in the films of the new 'transnational' directors Jackie Chan, John Woo and Ang Lee.

By introducing a strict quota system and severe censorship of Western films, China has done much to eliminate contemporary offences. Ironically, it is Chinese film-makers who are now accused of bringing China into disrepute by presenting negative portrayals of China and its problems. Directors are accused not just of flouting Chinese cultural norms by representing immoral and criminal behaviour but are guilty of the cardinal sin of *jia chou bu ke wai yang* or washing dirty linen in public. Films apparently made for foreign tastes which appear to be selling oriental exoticism to a Western audience is seen as cultural betrayal which is all the more painful because it comes from within.

Case study: To Live

Adapted from Yu Hua's 1992 novel, *To Live* (1994) is a vivid account of one family's struggle through three decades of political upheaval. Heavily criticised by the State censors, it presented an overview of Chinese rule under Mao Zedong.

The film opens in the late 1940s, with Xu Fugui gambling away his family estate. Deserted by his wife, Jiazhen, and thrown out of his house, he is forced to live on the streets of Shanghai. Only when he has proven he has given up gambling does Jiazhen return to him with their daughter, Fengxia, and newly born son Youqing. Borrowing a collection of shadow play puppets, Fugui and friend Chunsheng tour the provinces. Captured by Guomindang soldiers, they are liberated by the Red Army, and after fighting for the Communist cause, return home heroes of the revolution.

During his absence, Jiazhen and her children have had to find any means to escape destitution. Though suffering the hardships of poverty, Fugui claims that in the current political climate, 'It's good to be poor'. His opinion is reinforced by the execution of the man who tricked Fugui out of his family estate, whose position in society placed him among the landed classes and was therefore seen as an enemy of the people.

Progressing to 1958 and the implementation of the Great Leap Forward, Fugui is increasingly worried by the increase of party interference in people's lives, generating paranoia and fear of the state apparatus. The authorities have set targets for each town to collect a specific amount of iron to use in the battle to 'liberate' Taiwan. Kitchen utensils are confiscated and everyone is required to eat at the communal kitchens. When the town surpasses its target, children are invited to attend the official smelting down of the iron. News also spreads of the imminent arrival of the district chief. Afraid that his family will be seen as unpatriotic if any member fails to attend, Fugui forces a tired Youqing to go to the smelting. Unfortunately, Youqing is killed in an accident involving the district chief's car. The chief attends Youqing's burial and Fugai is shocked to see it is Chunsheng.

It is June 1966 and the Cultural Revolution has just begun. Fugui is persuaded by the town leader to destroy his puppets for fear that they would be seen as an anti-Communist artefact whose characters were 'classic feudal types'. As the chief states, 'The older, the more revolutionary'. Both the town chief and Chunsheng face charges of being a capitalist lackey, which will result either in their imprisonment or execution. Following her betrothal and wedding to Erxi, an active participant of the

Cultural Revolution, Fengxia is admitted to hospital to give birth to their first child. On arrival at the hospital, Fugui and Jiazhen discover that all doctors have been imprisoned for being an elite class, leaving only inexperienced nurses in charge. Out of fear for her safety, Erxi and Fugui manage to secure the release of a doctor to oversee the birth. Having not eaten for days, the doctor feasts on steamed buns which rupture his stomach, killing him before he can save Fengxia, who haemorrhages chronically following the birth of her son. The film ends a few years later, with Fugui, Jiazhen and Little Bun, Fengxia's son, visiting the grave of his mother and uncle, and paying homage to those who lost their lives as China tried to rebuild itself.

To Live was heavily criticised by the Chinese government for its negative portrayal of life during Mao's regime. Although popular in the West, winning the Grand Jury Prize at the Cannes Film Festival, its director Zhang Yimou was heavily censured. In paralleling the major events of China's history following the Communist uprising, he questioned the achievements of Mao's industrial and cultural policies.

Each of the four periods depicted in the film, the one prior to Communist rule and the three that lead up to the time just prior to Mao's death, contrast how one family struggled to survive within the changing social fabric of Chinese society. Though critical of Communist policies, the film also attacked the status quo of Chiang Kai-shek's rule, in particular, the abasement of women, who were powerless in a society dominated by Confucian values. At the beginning of the film, Jiazhen is unable to stop her husband's gambling. On her one attempt to save her family's fortune, when she visits the gambling house to ask Fugui to accompany her and her daughter home, she is publicly humiliated. Even by leaving him, Jiazhen risks becoming a social outcast. Her return to Fugui may be little to do with the desire to be back with her reformed husband than her inability to survive outside the family structure, no matter how intolerable the situation.

In the period following the Communist victory, women are seen to have a more active role in society. Although the remnants of China's feudal and Confucian past remain embedded within the grassroots of Chinese society, women are no longer subject to the strict constraints of life that existed prior to Mao's rule. Jiazhen's sense of independence is seen to be much stronger in Fengxia and although she lacks a voice, through a childhood illness, Jiazhen's daughter is an assertive and active member of the Cultural Revolution.

However, whatever progress was made on the part of women during Mao's rule, Chinese society is seen to continue in its suffering: progress is mirrored by tragedy within the family. The film questions the price at which each target was reached. The smelting of metal, which supplied the armouries fighting in Taiwan, is linked to the death of Youquing. The link is compounded, not only by his death being caused by the reckless driving of the district chief of the Communist Party, but that the chief happens to be Fugui's closest friend. Thus the personal and political are inextricably linked, with the latter imposing an increasing strain on the lives of ordinary Chinese people.

This link continues in the film's final section. The Cultural Revolution was introduced to better the lot of the underprivileged throughout China, but did more harm than good. The detaining of doctors as capitalist lackeys and members of an elitist class, replacing them with inexperienced, untrained nurses, results in the death of Fengxia. In a bitter irony, Erxi manages to secure the release of a malnourished doctor, who kills himself through over-eating before he is able to save Fengxia's life.

Each period also shows an increase of paranoia amongst the Chinese people. When Youquing plays a practical joke in the communal kitchen, on a boy who was bullying his sister, the boy's father accuses him of sabotaging the Great Leap Forward. Fugui's irrational fear of official reprisals forces him to beat his son in front of the crowd. Similarly, it is his fear of the family not being seen to do its duty that begins the chain of events leading to Youquing's death. As Fugui states, 'Smelting steel is everyone's duty. We can't be politically backward.'

The historical bonds of family and community also decreases through each of the periods following 1949. The film uses entertainment to reflect the changing environment. Whereas the shadow plays are initially seen to present scenes of familial and feudal strife, the stories gradually become more politicised. When Fugui and his troupe perform in front of the Red Army during the revolution, the stories are more traditional, but restructured to tell tales of honour and heroism amongst soldiers fighting with Mao. Later, after Fugui has been forced to destroy his puppets, which have become symbols of China's capitalist past, the wedding party attending the marriage of Fengxia and Erxi sing a 'traditional' Communist song, which praises Mao as being 'dearer than mother and father'. As with the songs appropriated by the Communist Party in *Yellow Earth* (1984), which will be examined in Chapter 3, everything, including the family, has become subservient to the rule of central government.

2   THE NEW WAVE

The State film industry underwent a radical change following the death of Mao in 1976 and the subsequent overthrow of the Gang of Four in 1977. As part of Deng Xiaoping's 'Four Modernisations' campaign, the Cultural Revolution models of film-making were abandoned in favour of a more topical cinema. The two main legacies of film history in China – the humanist-realist tradition of the 1940s, and the socialist-realist tradition of the Cultural Revolution – combined with a new atmosphere of liberalism. Throughout the 1980s these films examined social problems without the formulaic solutions offered by the films of the 1960s and 1970s. One of the best known is *Hibiscus Town* (1986), about the effects on relationships and lifestyles of people in a remote town during the Cultural Revolution. The political upheavals and government policies are heavily criticised in the film in a way that would not have been tolerated a decade before. Films were also made with a foreign audience in mind, such as *Savage Land* (1981) about a revenge killing by an escaped convict, and *Regret for the Past* (1981) in which a marriage founders in the face of social opposition in pre-Revolutionary China. The traumatic experiences of the Cultural Revolution, increasing exposure to Western films and a constructive role played by the Beijing Film Academy contributed to a 'new vibrancy' which heralded the work of the Fifth Generation directors (see Tam & Dissanayake 1998).

The new wave movement in mainland Chinese films coincided with the release of the first films made by the graduating class of 1982 from the Beijing Film Academy. China's only film-teaching school had newly reopened in 1978 having been closed, like the majority of educational institutions in China, at the start of the Cultural Revolution. Following fierce competition, the hundred places in its departments were filled by a talented group who were to become known as the Fifth Generation of film-makers in China, so-named because of their place in Chinese film history and because they were mainly comprised of members from the fifth class to graduate from the school's Directing Department.

The previous generations are not so easily defined. In broad terms we can categorise these as follows. Firstly, there were the early pioneers of cinema at the beginning of the twentieth century. Then came their successors, such as Shi Dongshan, who mostly directed martial arts films, who developed the industry in the 1920s. The third generation were made up of the film-makers who presided over the so-called 'Golden Age' of Chinese films in the 1930s and 1940s, including Cai Chusheng whose *Song of the Fishermen* (1935) was the first Chinese film to win a major international prize at the Moscow Film Festival and who, in 1947, co-directed the war epic *A Spring River Flows East* with Zheng Junli. Zheng also made the famous social satire *Crows and Sparrows* (1949), set in eve-of-Republic Shanghai. Finally, there was the 'Fourth Generation' of film-makers who had directed the Soviet-inspired propagandist films of the early Mao years, and included Lu Ban, director of *New Heroes and Heroines* (1951), and those who directed the 'new model operas' commissioned by Mao's ex-actress wife, Jiang Qing. Across these periods were directors whose work reflected the times in which they were made. The most well known is Xie Jin, who made *Woman Basketball Player No 5* (1957), *Stage Sisters* (1965) and *Hibiscus Town* (1986).

The early Fifth Generation films were characterised by stark locations and methods of representation in which landscape and ethnic minority groups figured consistently. They invited an altogether different kind of audience response from what Rey Chow calls 'three decades of propaganda-filled media' (Chow 1995: 26) which had gone before. They adopted a style characterised by a new film language, often recalling traditional Chinese painting, with a distinctive use of narrative structure and a focus on the questioning of Chinese culture itself. It was a decided break away from the formulaic films based on Soviet models, with their 'people's heroes' making impossible sacrifices for the common good.

A major theme of these earlier texts is an obsession with Chinese culture and customs. A deeply conservative film industry, constrained by tough censorship, was then invaded by a new generation of film-makers who shared the same life experiences. Such was the shortage of trained directors in the studios that they were able to start directing straight away, whereas in the past it was not unusual for a director to have to wait 20 years before his first solo opportunity. The decade-long political upheaval had left these fledgling directors with a powerful wish to express their feelings about themselves, their country and their culture.

One of the defining characteristics of these films is their ambiguity, or openness to audience interpretation. This in itself is a clear break from a tradition of didactic film-making which had dominated Chinese cinema mostly because 'ambiguity ... by various strategies refuses either to set up a clear moral/political position for the viewer or to construct an exemplary positive or negative figure for emulation or criticism' (Browne *et al.* 1994: 10). The films are thus positioned to invite analytical reading that demands independent thought by the audience.

Film was not the only art form asking these questions. At the end of the 'ten chaotic years' of the Cultural Revolution, the theme of national identity emerged in 'search for roots' literary texts as well as in cinema in the 1970s and 1980s. The focus of intellectual enquiry in general changed, and the intelligentsia began 'asking themselves the big questions of the day: what is culture, what is our duty to civilisation, what must we do about this great sinking ship called the Chinese nation?' (Zha 1994: 32). Film-makers shared these concerns, and the traditional practice of adapting existing novels and short stories for film scripts, which the Fifth Generation directors followed, places the films firmly within this context.

In many ways, this was an attempt to discover how the inhumanities of the persecutions – particularly those perpetrated by 'ordinary' Chinese upon friends, neighbours, and even members of their own families – could have occurred. They sought to confirm or deny that Chinese culture was indeed 'a diseased body': in part it was a searching for a way forward in the face of the unacceptability of the Western model of development, 'an anxiety in the new era of openness, as the overwhelming presence of the Western other is increasingly felt' (Wang 1989: 34). This 'otherness' has become more vividly imminent as a result of recent openness to foreign culture, fuelled by Deng Xiaoping's economic reforms and the need to attract Western capital. Following centuries of relatively well-founded mistrust of foreign imperialist incursions, 'Westernness' became all the more threatening to a sense of national identity. The films of the Fifth Generation film-makers thus looks to the past for the roots of cultural crisis, discovers the reasons why change is resisted, but cannot formulate a way forward.

Fifth Generation directors

Fifth Generation directors focus their interest on the structure of a society which resists change. Whether narrative in the films concerns contemporary life, the past, or minority communities, they record the mundane details of everyday life and traditional practices. However, it is exactly this emphasis on the 'atemporal dimension of history' (Ma 1988: 24) that helps the viewer establish connections between the past and the present. Whether obsessively depicting the feudal past or narratives of life in remote rural areas, the central cultural dilemma addressed by these film-makers is that of being caught between the tyranny of this feudal past and an apparently spiritless commodity-orientated future.

The first Fifth Generation films originated from the tiny Guangxi Studio, in mid-southwest China, near the border with Vietnam. Mostly set in the barren regions of west China, they acquired the classification of 'Western films', where 'the simplicity and rawness of life provide a fertile ground for cultural critique and exploring questions of existence, meaning, and history, questions not sanctioned by a state intent on using film as an instrument for moral-political education' (Mayfair 2001: 36). *One and Eight*

(1984), the first Fifth Generation film to be completed at the studio, told of an incident during the Anti-Japanese war. A group of prisoners, who are granted their freedom to protect themselves, re-discover their patriotism, but not before director Zhang Junzhao critiques the role played by the Communist army during the conflict. Elsewhere, Wu Ziniu directed another drama set during the Anti-Japanese war, *Secret Decree* (1984), at the Xiaoxiang Film Studio, while Hu Mei directed *Army Nurse* (1985) for Beijing's August First Studio.

An examination of the life and work of three leading directors of the Fifth Generation, a selection of whose films are analysed in more detail elsewhere in the book, shows how their concerns and methods coincided to form a recognisable body of work that differed greatly from China's output over the preceding thirty years.

Chen Kaige

Chen Kaige, the best known of the Fifth Generation directors, was born in 1952 in Beijing, into a family already steeped in the traditions of film-making. His father was Chen Huaikai, a successful director of Chinese Opera films at the Beijing Film Studio, and his mother was a script editor. In 1966, his schooling ended with the outbreak of the Cultural Revolution and two years later he was sent to Yunnan Province in the far southwest of China, together with a number of his classmates. Initially working on a rubber plantation, he transferred to the army, an alternative form of service offered by the State to its urban youths. Five years later, he returned to Beijing to work in a factory and began his studies at the recently re-opened Film Academy and spent the years 1978–82 there. At first assigned to Beijing Film Studio, he was soon invited to join fellow graduate Zhang Yimou at the small Guangxi Film Studio, an invitation authorised by both studios, as the former was over-populated with new directors, whereas the more remote studio lacked skilled technicians. The result of his collaboration with Zhang, whose cinematography on *One and Eight* helped define the look of the new wave of Chinese film-makers, was *Yellow Earth* (1984). Attacked by the older members of the film establishment, the film garnered favourable reviews abroad and was a success with a mainly Chinese audience at the 1985 Hong Kong Film Festival.

Yellow Earth was filmed on location on the Loess Plateau of the North Shaanxi Province, where legend has it that Xuanyuan, the first Chinese emperor is buried, and in more recent years, where the Long March ended and Mao Zedong drew up his plans for a new Chinese nation. Adapted from Ke Lan's popular novel, 'Echo in the Deep Valley', the film dealt with resistance to change in a peasant community. Like *One and Eight*, the film was greatly enhanced by the cinematography of Zhang Yimou. However, the collaboration only lasted through to Chen's second film, *The Big Parade* (1985). Filmed once again through the aegis of the Guangxi Film Studio, it drew on Chen's experience of army comradeship to address important questions not only about conditions for conscripts but the purpose and nature of authority and military service. Such was the severity of Chen's view that censors demanded the final scene be re-shot. The image of an empty Tiananmen Square, replacing the show of military might that the whole film had been building up to, was too nihilistic an ending for the authorities, no matter how metaphorically expressed it was.

In *King of the Children* (1987), made for Xi'an Film Studio, and for which Chen received his first writing credit with Wan Zhi, raising questions of command and authority in terms of education. A conscripted teacher in a remote village raises doubts over the value of rote-learning of the classics, instead of new explorations into the role of education in a transformed society. Elliptical in its storytelling, and ethereal in the way the Yunnan landscape is presented, the film was seen to distance an already small domestic audience. However, Chen once again won acclaim from international critics and festival audiences. Having already earned the nickname 'Fake Mandarin' for what audiences saw as the seemingly meandering narrative structure and wanton obscurity of his work, Chen directed his most allegorical film to date, the internationally financed *Life on a String* (1991). The tale of a peripatetic blind lute player and his young assistant wandering across vast plains whilst waiting for the breaking of the symbolic thousandth string on his instrument, it brought bewilderment to audiences otherwise stunned by the beauty of its images.

FIGURE 1 *Farewell My Concubine*

It was with his next film that Chen both cemented his reputation for spectacle and deeply offended the Chinese censors. *Farewell My Concubine* (1993), made for Beijing Film Studio with finance from Hong Kong and starring Gong Li, dealt with sensitive issues such as homosexuality, opium addiction, prostitution and child abuse. However, it was the scenes of persecution during the Cultural Revolution that earned it an outright ban. Chen subsequently agreed to be interviewed at length for Stanley Kwan's *Yang + Yin: Gender in Chinese Cinema* (1996), and explained some of the decisions he had made in adapting the script of *Farewell My Concubine*, particularly certain narrative elements that provoked accusations of homophobia. Nevertheless, it went on to become the first Chinese film to win an Academy Award.

Lavish spectacle has since become the mainstay of Chen's output. His subsequent film, *Temptress Moon* (1996), recreates China in the 1920s as it follows the disintegration of a wealthy but dysfunctional family. Starring Gong Li and Leslie Cheung, and photographed by Wong Kar-wai regular Christopher Doyle, the film possesses a dreamy quality deserving of its tale of opium addiction, and shows a genuine interest in sexual passion, previously missing from Chen's work.

His most recent Chinese film, *The Emperor and the Assassin* (1999), is the most expensive film ever made in Asia, with a $20 million budget. Chen's weakest film to date, it tells of the power struggle surrounding Ying Zheng, China's first emperor. Re-treading ground already covered by Zhou Xiaowen in *The Emperor's Shadow* (1996), it is an overblown epic, memorable more for its immense battle scenes than it is for its insights into those times, or any parallels with contemporary Chinese society.

Since the late 1980s, Chen has spent more time in the West. He embarked on a lecture tour in America in 1988 and is current filming in London. *Killing Me Softly* (due for release in 2002) traces the obsessive relationship between a research scientist and a mysterious mountaineer. Starring Heather Graham and Joseph Fiennes, Chen appears to have turned his back on his Chinese cinema for the time being.

Tian Zhuangzhuang

Tian Zhuangzhuang was also born in 1952 to a family with close connections to the film industry. His mother, Yu Lan, had been a film star and became head of the Beijing Children's Film Studio. His father, Tian Tang, was an actor and Vice-President of the Ministry of Culture's Film Bureau. As a result, Tian was able to attend many censorship screenings in his youth. He was sent to Jilin Province in 1968, again under Mao's scheme for evacuating urban youths to the countryside in order to experience a peasant life. His parents meanwhile were imprisoned as 'rightists' and intellectuals. Like Chen, he eventually joined the army, managing to train as a photographer and then as a cinematographer at the Beijing Agricultural Studio, after returning to civilian life in 1975. Like Chen Kaige, he was admitted to the directors' class at Beijing Film Academy in 1978 and graduated in 1982.

His debut film, *On the Hunting Ground* (1984), a documentary-style feature about the enigmatic hunting codes of Mongolian plainsmen, attracted critical attention yet sold only four prints, incurring huge losses for the Inner Mongolian Film Studio. *Horse Thief* (1985) alienated Chinese audiences but gained recognition abroad. Described by Tian as being about 'the relation-ships between humanity and religion, and between humanity and nature' (Berry 1991: 128), the film tells the story, through stark imagery and little dialogue, of a thief whose actions bring shame upon his tribe and disaster upon his family. Almost hallucinatory in the way it depicts the ceaseless rit-uals of the tribespeople's rural existence, Tian attracted criticism for claim-ing that his films' lack of appeal amongst contemporary audiences was because he was making films for 'audiences of the next century to watch'. He also composed the sparse music for the film, as he had done for *King of the Children* and *Life on a String*.

Following his forays into ethnographic cinema, Tian made a number of attempts to work within the mainstream. His *Rock n'Roll Kids* (1988), made for the Youth Film Studio, was successfully aimed at the urban youth market, and *Li Lianying: The Imperial Eunuch* (1991) resembles popular historical epics.

It was with *The Blue Kite* (1993), which reflected his admiration for the Italian Neo-realists, Taiwanese director Hou-Hsiao Hsien and Japan's Yasu-jiro Ozu, that Tian finally found critical and commercial success. A popular hit at international film festivals, it won admiration with foreign audiences for its compassionate portrayal of an ordinary Beijing family enduring the effects of the Cultural Revolution. It was not given a general release in China because of its severe criticism of government measures, presented through ironic imagery and low-key performances by the actors representing the beleaguered family. Tian was officially banned from making any more films until 1996 and now mostly works as a producer, encouraging new directors.

Zhang Yimou

Zhang Yimou, born in 1950 near Xi'an in Shaanxi province, also joined the ranks of the millions of urban youths sent to work in remote country dis-tricts during the Cultural Revolution. Admitted to the Beijing Film Academy in 1978, he was assigned to the cinematography training school. On grad-uation he was posted to the small Guangxi Film Studio, and soon found himself working on *One and Eight* with director Zhang Junzhao. Supportive studio chief Wu Tianming then allowed him to enlist fellow-graduate Chen Kaige to direct *Yellow Earth*. Both films, and Zhang's second film with Chen, *The Big Parade* (1985), displayed a stark visual style that contrasted with what had come before it. In 1996, Yimou stepped in front of the camera for the first time, in Lao Jing's *Old Well* (1986), which won him the Best Actor award at the Tokyo Film Festival.

Zhang's first film as director, *Red Sorghum* (1988), set in a remote north-eastern region, won the Golden Bear award at the 1988 Berlin Film Festival and was hugely popular in China. It became a cult film amongst Chinese youths for its earthy upbeat portrayal of the main protagonist and its strong nationalist thread. The film also marked the debut of Gong Li, whose success grew with the critical popularity of the Fifth Generation directors and has since become China's leading film actress.

Zhang's next film as director, *Codename Cougar* (1989), was originally intended as an exploration of the relationship between Chinese and Taiwanese authorities, but due to the sensitivity of the subject matter and severe censorial control, the film became nothing more than an unexceptional action thriller. For his next two films, Zhang returned to the central theme of *Red Sorghum*: the sale of women into marriage. Exquisitely shot, *Ju Dou* (1990) and *Raise the Red Lantern* (1991) owe much to Japanese masters Yasujiro Ozu and Kenji Mizoguchi in terms of their beguilingly sparse visual style. Both films won international acclaim at film festivals and were outstandingly successful art-house releases in America, but were refused a release in China. The ban was subsequently lifted in 1992 following Deng Xiaoping's tour of south China when he called for a speed-up of reform and liberalisation. *Ju Dou*, which will be a case study later in the book, tells the story of a woman who embarks on a relationship with her abusive husband's nephew. A coruscating account of a woman's lot in 1920s rural China, it once again featured Gong Li in the title role and was more explicit in its use of sexual imagery. *Raise the Red Lantern* was more restrained than Zhang's previous work, but displayed a maturity and development of his formal style. Gong Li plays a young student who ignores her mother's objections and agrees to become the fourth wife of a wealthy clan leader.

FIGURE 2 *Raise the Red Lantern*

Arousing the jealousy of the other wives, she soon finds out that the only person with power is the husband, and the women are merely pawns, on hold to satisfy his whims. Zhang's static camera captures both the claustrophobia of the wives' surroundings and the state of suspension in which they are kept.

Overseas producers were increasingly keen to invest in Zhang's films, offering better pay, high technical standards and some measure of protection from Film Bureau decisions. Although they could ban or delay release of his films in China, foreign money bought distribution rights abroad. However, with *The Story of Qiu Ju* (1992), Zhang appeared to be making amends for previous offences. Shot in an impressive *cinéma verité* style, achieved by using hidden cameras and a cast almost entirely comprised of non-actors, it won the Grand Jury Prize at Venice in 1992, with Gong Li being awarded Best Actress. The film, about an ordinary peasant woman's search for justice, was praised by the Chief of the Propaganda Ministry himself.

It seemed to pay tribute not only to Chinese womanhood but to China's judiciary reforms. The Propaganda Minister apparently missed the significance of the final freeze-frame close-up of Qiu Ju's dismayed face as the head of the village is arrested. With typical ambiguity, Zhang suggests that a remote and bureaucratic justice system is irrelevant to the realities of village co-dependencies.

Zhang reinstated his status as agent provocateur of Chinese cinema with *To Live* (1994). Its satirical portrayal of the effects of government policy was unlikely to pass the censors and Zhang had the film smuggled to Cannes, where it won two Foreign Language Film awards. However, its criticism of Chinese society under Mao resulted in official condemnation from the Chinese authorities whose strict censure nearly cut short the director's career. As punishment, Zhang was banned from making films for five years and the shooting of his next project, *Shanghai Triad* (1995), was halted. Gong Li was barred from attending foreign film festivals and told to give no newspaper interviews. This decision was later rescinded – partly, it has been suggested, because Zhang showed the necessary level of contrition, and also because of the film's positive reception in the West.

When completed, *Shanghai Triad* was a return to less controversial subject-matter, with the tale of a 1930s nightclub entertainer-cum-gangster's moll redeemed by a brief pastoral idyll before her tragic end. Lacking the depth and narrative coherence of his better work, Zhang's vivid use of colour nevertheless ensures the film is more than merely watchable.

Keep Cool (1997) marked a radical departure for the director. A light-hearted contemporary comedy, that draws heavily from the frenetic style of Hong Kong cinema, Zhang abandoned his formalism for hand-held cameras and, following the end of their long-running and controversial affair, worked without Gong Li. Jiang Wen plays a bookseller whose girlfriend suddenly leaves him for a richer man. Unable to come to terms with the end of the relationship, he scours Beijing in search of her, with hilarious results. Although entered for the Cannes Film Festival, *Keep Cool* was withdrawn from competition and Zhang was prevented from attending, because the Chinese authorities objected to the inclusion of Martin Scorsese's Tibetan epic, *Kundun* (1997).

Zhang's two most recent films have received financial backing from the Sony Corporation. *Not One Less* (1999), which won Zhang another Golden Lion at the Venice Film Festival, combines unswerving realism in its portrait of the problems of rural education and an unconvincing happy ending that seems more inspired by contemporary Hollywood. *The Road Home* (2000) is a return to the films made by pre-Fifth Generation directors such as Xie Jin. Set in the present day, with flashbacks to the 1950s, the film charts the relationship between a village girl and a young teacher seconded to the local school. Claiming that contemporary Chinese could be as noble as previous generations if they only pay more attention to traditions, the film sits uneasily next to his previous work. Unlike many of his contemporaries, he says he has no intention of leaving for the West, relying on Chinese social concerns for his inspiration.

Film censorship

In 1949, when Mao Zedong established the Communist Party government in China, the China Film Bureau was instituted under the Ministry of Culture, together with a Ministry of Propaganda, subsequently becoming part of a Ministry of Television and Radio Broadcasting and Film in 1986. The Film Bureau controls all other units associated with making, processing and distributing films. There are 22 major studios in China and many smaller units in 29 provinces and municipalities, of which 16 have approval from the Film Bureau to make feature films.

The China Film Bureau not only has censorial control and gives 'letters of approval' to scripts, which must be submitted before filming begins, but calls annual meetings for studio heads to discuss production quotas, categories of film, policies and regulations, and works out long-term plans for the development of the film industry as well as dealing with foreign exchanges and film agreements abroad. This intimate link with the entire process means that the Bureau may not only ask for changes in scripts as well as in completed films, it can certify a film for release only within China and, if need be, to a limited audience, or it may approve a film for international distribution. The Import and Export division of the China

Film Corporation attends about 70 of the major international festivals and enters China's best films. All films made in China are required to be sent for 'inspection' but films from the August First Film Studio, which makes recruitment and training films for the armed forces, must initially go through central military censorship. With the exception of the chief of the Film Bureau, most members of the censorship board are from outside the film industry but responsible to higher levels of the Party/State structure.

The Party Committee of any studio is expected to act to make sure films do not run counter to government policy. The restrictions on nudity, graphic violence and sexual acts is well known, but it is the portrayal of adverse social conditions, interpreted as criticism of government policy, which has predominantly concerned the censors and which is a source of conflict between the authorities and film-makers. Control methods are rigorous and extensive: aside from cuts made to finished films, bans on home distribution and/or export, films can be retained or the censorship board can demand months of re-shooting. It can also delay release of a film until the subject matter seems outdated or at least no longer controversial.

For their part, film-makers have long complained of the lack of an explicit film code. International status protects many directors from outright bans, not least because they bring prestige and financial gain to a struggling industry. There are harsher punishments, however: negatives may be seized, directors forbidden to travel, films blacklisted as part of an official protest against another film, and future permits jeopardised. Blacklisting has often been used to curb the activities of the most persistent independent film-makers. In April 1994, in a major crackdown, seven directors who had made and distributed 'illegal' films were blacklisted. The government sent directives to the country's official studios, processing labs and equipment rental services, forbidding contact with the listed personnel, or giving assistance in any form. The reason given was that these film-makers worked 'outside the official parameter'.

Restricting co-productions is an additional measure for controlling foreign input. Funding gives leverage to other countries in negotiating the final form and distribution of the film, as well as a share of revenue, although it is an important source of finance for Chinese film-makers. In 1997, new regulations stipulated a maximum of 25 per cent investment per annum through international co-production. Film festival pressure is a high-profile method for the Chinese authorities to restrict screenings. Additionally, directors of 'sensitive' films have often been prevented from attending international film festivals, either by 'persuasion' or by the more extreme measure of passport confiscation.

Actually preventing films being made is a comparatively rare form of control but can be achieved by pressuring the financiers of independent film-makers. China's action against dissident film-makers is curbed to an extent by a wish for foreign approval. The Film Bureau seems unwilling to act directly against film-makers by legal action. The international visibility of their work protects them, so that officially 'banned' films like Zhang Yuan's *Beijing Bastards* (1993) and *Postman* (1995), directed by He Yi (aka Jia Zhanke), are seen by Tony Rayns as 'bargaining chips in the struggle for a genuine freedom of expression in China' (Rayns 1995: 79). Since the late 1980s, questions of business interests in the global markets also greatly influence film policy abroad. Following the success of *The Lion King* (1994) at Chinese theatres in 1995, the Walt Disney Company released Martin Scorsese's *Kundun*, about the early life of the Dalai Lama, even at the risk of jeopardising future business interests in China.

Recently, the most influential factor in film production has been economics. Films need to appeal to an audience who increasingly demand well-crafted American or Hong Kong entertainment films. However, recent changes in funding have caused problems for the film studios. Before Deng Xiaoping came to power in 1979, Chinese film studios completed films according to annual plans designed by the Film Bureau. For each film all studios were paid the same, regardless of costs or box-office receipts. In 1980, with the loosening of controls, studios could censor their own scripts but the final product still had to be submitted to the Film Bureau. However, studios are reluctant to risk film-making only to have a project banned, so resort to renting out studios for revenue. Increased censorship after the Tiananmen events of 1989 and rising television ownership seriously affected mass cinema audience. Between 1979 and 1991 admissions fell by 50 per cent, reducing the number of prints needed and likewise therefore the income from the State, although box-office income doubled during this period.

In 1994, new regulations removed the obligation of producers within China to sell their films to the China Film Corporation. Furthermore, the question of the status of Hong Kong film-makers is not settled, since everyone involved in the mainland film industry is aware of the potentially enormous effect of wealthy Hong Kong film-makers, now no longer classed as 'foreigners', having free access to participation throughout the industry after 1997. Private funding as a source of film investment is increasing and has long been a practice in independent filming. In response to studio pressure, in July 1997 the Ministry finally implemented the new Film Administration Regulations which state that the Film Bureau will in future explain why a film has been banned and be explicit about the changes required before release as well as giving reasons for retaining projects. The report is to be in writing and delivered within thirty days of a film's submission to avoid costly and frustrating delays.

Case study: The Blue Kite

Contrary to his ethnographic accounts of minority groups living in the Chinese hinterland – *On the Hunting Ground* and *Horse Thief* – *The Blue Kite* tells the story of an 'ordinary' Chinese family living in Beijing and experiencing the effects of political upheavals. Set mainly in a courtyard and adjacent house in a Beijing back-street, the film charts the years between 1953 (the death of Stalin) to 1966 (the outbreak of the Cultural Revolution). The film is narrated from the point of view of a small boy, Tietou, who sees the disastrous effects on his family of various government directives. The blue kite motif appears at intervals throughout the film as a symbol of domestic happiness: fragile, and constantly in need of rebuilding. In its portrayal of the trials and upheavals of an era through the vicissitudes of one family, Tian Zhuangzhuang's film embodies a comprehensive indictment of the effects of the Cultural Revolution on ordinary

FIGURE 3 *The Blue Kite*

people. The 'Mother Courage' figure of the thrice-widowed heroine is the film's main sufferer, as her husbands fall victim one by one to the troubles of the times.

Early in the film, the importance of social class is ironically underlined when the mother, an ex-teacher married to a librarian, expresses disappointment upon learning that the family are not, after all, to be redesignated as 'working class' – the only desirable, indeed the only safe, class in Mao's China. The absurdity of reversals in social status is highlighted in a scene where her husband tells her with unaffected pleasure that the library has won the district award for manual labour. Tietou's uncle Shuyan, who complains about the examination system at his school in response to the invitation to criticise during the Hundred Flowers period, is sent to work on the land, whilst Tietou's father, Shaolong, who becomes a scapegoat of the need to root out 'rightists' is sent to a labour camp where he dies. Meanwhile, Tietou's other uncle, Shusheng, contracts an eye disease, about the only disaster not attributable to government policy, and his girlfriend suffers a reversal to her career when she refuses to act

FIGURE 4 *The Blue Kite*

as an 'escort' at dances put on for Party officials. These events contrast with the humanity and charity shown to one another by the 'ordinary' characters: the colleague responsible for the librarian's designation as rightist tries to make amends to the family in his absence and eventually marries the widow; a party cadre assures a 'landlady' suspected of hoarding food that some celebration dumplings will be returned once 'an example' has been registered and the cadre has been seen to carry out her duties.

When her second husband dies from a combination of overwork and poor diet, the mother is again forced by economic circumstances to marry, this time to an elderly academic whose social position seems secure: he is a Communist Party official. In a violent climactic scene, he too falls victim, this time to the Red Guards who have been instructed to destroy all the old signs of class privilege – in this case the possession of a comfortable house and a number of books. The overthrow of traditional authority and the adverse effects on young people is depicted in a scene where Tietou gleefully relates how students joined in beating the headmistress – and receives a blow from his appalled mother. One critic appropriately describes it as a 'film about a trust betrayed: the trust of people who believed in a wise and benevolent leadership' (Kemp 1994: 55).

Anonymous letters were sent to the Party Central Committee during the shooting of the film and the studio banned post-production in Japan, but it was completed a year later with finance from a Dutch company and premiered at Cannes in 1993. China boycotted the Festival, but the film won prizes for Best Film and Best Actress. The authorities were reportedly so furious at the finished result, already delivered to Hong Kong for the post-production phase, that Tian was prevented from leaving to edit in Hong Kong. The film was finished in March 1992 but post-production was delayed by the censors, and eventually completed in Japan from the director's notes. The film was then smuggled to Cannes, and later provoked a walk-out at Tokyo where the Chinese said they would prosecute film-makers for making films 'without permission'. Sources close to the film have said that the allusions to the sexual proclivities of Party leaders was one of the main reasons Chinese cultural bureaucrats have tried to prevent the film's release at home and screenings at festivals abroad (see Schilling 1993).

Xiao Mao's script for *The Blue Kite* is based on Tian's own family history. It had become an obsession of the director's because he felt many people did not know the real story of what happened during the years depicted: 'Discussion of the persecutions of the anti-rightist campaigns that followed the Hundred Flowers policy is still taboo for writers, artists and film-makers' (Vidal-Hall 1995: 80).

Following what he describes as 'a childhood of broken dreams' (Remy 1994: 28) when he was sent to Manchuria, spending five years in the army while his parents were imprisoned as 'rightists', Tian is reportedly disappointed that the young people of present-day China are not interested in the past, but only in 'catching up' with the West.

3   DISSIDENCE AND DISGUISE

As the previous chapter has shown, Fifth Generation directors rarely engaged with contemporary events head on – they would have little chance of getting beyond the censorship board's script-approval stage. Instead, their films addressed more generally the fundamental question of the relation of the individual to the State. At the same time they exposed traditional sources of power within Chinese society to international comment. With so much at stake, it is hardly surprising that relationships between film-makers and government in China consisted of a series of shifting moves and counter-moves, skirmishes and evasions, as both sides attempted to achieve their aim and represent conflicting realities.

It was the film-makers persistence, together with the portrayal of 'backward' feudalism, that attracted the unfavourable attention of the government. Their distinctive mode of film-making became threatening to those in power because the whole purpose of film, as advanced by the Fifth Generation directors, had changed. Influenced by European film-makers and movements, whose works they had been exposed to for the first time, they began to use film to express their individual thoughts and ideas. As Ma Ning puts it, 'films became for them a bridge between their subjectivity and the objective world' (Ma 1988: 24).

Like other intellectuals in the post-revolution period, the Fifth Generation directors questioned the origins of Chinese culture. Their films critiqued the nation's political and social dynamics especially where they constrained personal freedom and were the cause of suffering. As such, the films not only reflect culture, but raise awareness of the need for change. Their cinema, as Graham Turner observes, can be seen as a part of a continuing effort, ongoing through this century, at 'remaking China socially and economically' (Turner 1988: 137).

Although dissident tendencies in written texts were easily discovered and necessary steps were taken to suppress criticism in films, censorship was made increasingly difficult by the inherent ambiguity of the visual image. Supported by allegory, symbol and metaphor – components of traditional Chinese cultural expression – Fifth Generation films have had a degree of success in evading the censors. In the skilful manipulation of *mise-en-scène*, the films operate as an ironic or contrasting commentary to spoken words and narrative action on screen. The cultural knowledge of each film's audience ensured that the film-makers message was understood.

An understanding of metaphor and symbolism is essential in reading of the complexity of the film image. Metaphor can be defined as 'the presentation of one idea in terms of another, belonging to a different category', so that either our understanding of the first idea is transformed, or so that 'from the fusion of the two ideas a new one is created' (Whittock 1990: 5). The role of the audience is crucial in this respect. It is necessary for the mind, that is, the 'machine for making connections' (Martin 1975: 213) to associate images on the screen with their own experience, however indirect the association may be. The signification of the film image will be the product of many factors, including 'its place in social beliefs or customs, even its cultural and historical siting' (Whittock 1990: 3). Film is often thought of as having 'high international currency' in that films of very different cultural origins can be viewed with some degree of understanding by a variety of foreign audiences, but certain meanings are culture-specific and have little if anything to do with how images are perceived in combination or otherwise.

An example of this occurs in *The Blue Kite* in the scene where people take part in a bird-scaring campaign, as part of the Great Leap Forward initiative of 1957–58. The young Tietou joins enthusiastically in creating a noisy disturbance forcing seed-eating birds to remain airborne until they drop exhausted from the sky. At one point he catches a sparrow, which he immediately releases. There is no dialogue, but by this point in the film the idea of flying as a symbol of domestic happiness and escape from political oppression has been well established by the use of kite-flying, reinforced by other visual 'echoes'. The bird's temporary release is linked in the mind of the audience with the dominant motif of a film teeming with symbolism; the incident would also remind a Chinese audience that the bird-scaring campaign backfired because the resulting plague of insects produced lower-than-usual harvests and contributed to a famine in which millions starved. The entire scene becomes an allegory of oppression, with people 'scared' into compliance with a harsh regime which caused many to perish. This and other films depended on an audience that could access knowledge of cultural as well as cinematic codes to make their meanings apparent. The Chinese Film Censorship Board worked to excise this sort of criticism from films, and were sometimes beguiled by subtle use of these methods. Directors thus learned to develop a talent for negotiation and persuasion needed for survival as a film-maker in China.

The films also draw on other aspects of traditional Chinese pictorial art as a rich source of meaning. In Chinese painting, for instance, there is no tradition of perspective, but by applying a blend of Chinese art with modern technology Chinese film-makers have 'learned to rapidly adapt the ability of the camera lens to expose an immediate, concrete reality to the traditional techniques of Chinese poets and painters' (Woo 1991: 21). In traditional forms of painting and poetry, humanity is seen to be at one with 'all parts of nature' (Woo 1991: 22). There is an attempt to find a balance, a tranquillity between the two. This is particularly prevalent in the early films of the Fifth Generation, where the role of landscape is pivotal to the narrative. In *Horse Thief*, for example, the landscape is part of and reactive to, the character's lives. When the thief is banished from his tribe, it is as though nature has deserted him and he is forced to face the harshness of a barren landscape. Similarly, the shame endured by his tribe results in a famine that forces them to leave their homeland. A similar use of nature is employed in *Yellow Earth*, which will be discussed in more depth at the end of the chapter.

Colour symbolism is another important area for creating meaning in the films. The use of red dominates many of the Fifth Generation films. Described by Zhang Yimou as conveying 'a passionate attitude toward living, an unrestricted vitality ... and an emotionally spirited attitude toward human life' (Jiao 2001: 6), it has dominated the emotions at the core of all his early films. However, their meaning can also differ from Western conventions. In addition to desire, red is used – sometimes with ironic overtones – to signal happiness, whereas white is used for mourning.

A Chinese director automatically adopts the sentimental conventions familiar to Chinese poets and painters, such as a mother sewing for her son or the ritual of food offering and the significance of accepting presents to establish obligation or reconciliation. Gestures and body-language are another area where cultural knowledge is essential. A Western viewer may be perplexed by the apparent coldness of family relationships in China unless it is understood that affection is more usually shown by the actions described above than in words or physical touching. The figure of a man in a barren landscape does not necessarily signify loneliness so much as a sense of purpose in nature – a compositional feature that may be misread by a Western viewer.

Music plays an important role and many new wave films make extensive use of soundtrack themes and songs to structure narrative and characterisation. Sometimes obtrusively portentous, they can also be snatches of folk tunes or childhood songs with their own emotional associations for the audience. An almost hallucinatory effect, for instance, is achieved by the frequent repetition of the song in *The Story of Qiu Ju* when Qiu Ju sets out on the road yet again on her quest for justice. Another example is when the gangster's moll Bijou reveals an undeveloped side to her character, and encourages children to join her in singing a nursery rhyme, in *Shanghai Triad*. Traditional songs also play an integral role to the narrative of certain films. Both *Yellow Earth* and *Red Sorghum* use folk songs to describe social events such as marriage or annual festivities. In the case of the latter, a simple wedding song becomes both comical and threatening as a young bride-to-be is taken by porters to the home of her as-yet-unseen future husband.

The most significant cultural difference, however, lies in the director's expectations of the audience; unlike the tendency in Hollywood where the viewer's imagination is rarely intended to participate, and meaning is made relatively explicit, Chinese film very much depends on the active imaginative collaboration of its audience. The role of culturally defined codes and their implications – such as taking a shower, eating, working, travelling and gesture – are important as 'the specifically cinematic codes [which] together with the number of shared codes make up the syntax of the film' (Wollen 1972: 148). Given the complexity of the cinema image and the diversity of individual responses possible it is not surprising that the reception to the Fifth Generation directors' films has been so varied. The analysis of *Yellow Earth* later in this chapter will further illustrate the ambiguity of many images and the way in which the director is able to exploit this dimension of the film medium to provide a disguised form of social criticism.

The melodramatic imagination

The melodramatic tone of the Fifth Generation films is a characteristic that is still an obvious feature despite their break with the past in terms of style. Melodrama is a defining characteristic of Chinese films, and 'the melodramatic imagination is deeply rooted in Chinese life' (Pickowicz 1993: 325). Indeed, one of the most striking aspects of Fifth Generation film-making is the 'naturalistic' attention that is paid to the details of the domestic lives of the protagonists within the framework of the traditional melodrama. It reasserts the value of traditional peasant lifestyles and shows a shift in emphasis from the former 'model socialist' films with their emphasis on the world outside the home (see Dissanayake 1993).

One important influence is the films of director Xie Jin, China's most popular director, a transitional figure between earlier Chinese cinema and the new wave films of the 1980s. The concentration on women in extreme situations, for instance, is evident in films as far apart in time as 1954's *Rendezvous at Orchid Bridge* and *Hibiscus Town* from 1986. Condemned for his 'bourgeois' themes at the start of the Cultural Revolution, his films nevertheless 'illustrate the continuities in much of Chinese film-making' (Berry

1991: 198) and his critical attitude was a source of inspiration for the Fifth Generation directors.

There is a large element of allegory and symbolism within the melodramatic tradition. Ma Ning points to the frequent juxtaposition of country and city, tradition and modernisation as symbols for different sectors contending for domination as a prominent feature of Chinese cultural production in the 1980s (see Ma 1989). Furthermore, the characters in melodrama tend to stereotype and simplification instead of being individualised and complex, whereas the new wave films bring a psychological depth to lead characters, particularly with regard to women. The 'villain', however, is often a shadowy, indistinct or even unidentifiable figure, such as the husband only seen in long-shot in *Raise the Red Lantern*. If a cruel character is shown he (or she) is usually the agent of a more remote authority figure or institution. Typically, the oppressor has kindly impulses that are suppressed by the demands of tradition.

Problems in melodrama also tend to be clear and polarised instead of complex and multiple and this is characteristic of the new wave films where a specific problem presents itself at the outset and the rest of the film depicts the (usually unsuccessful) attempt to resolve it. In melodrama events occur unexpectedly, often bringing a reversal of fortune, and this is also characteristic of the new wave films that reflect, directly or indirectly, profound social upheavals. Settings in melodrama are often unusual and unfamiliar; the new wave films are characteristically set in remote areas or have a sense of isolated, even beleaguered circumstances. Melodrama also characteristically offers no solutions to problems but simply depicts events and their consequences and the new wave films have been criticised for their gloomy outcomes, leaving characters without redress for their sufferings or at best bewildered and resigned.

In the West, melodrama has been stigmatised as a relatively inferior, low-status genre, because of its association with popular or mass entertainment, and the fact that it takes the viewpoint of the victim, typically a woman, in a domestic setting. The plots of Victorian melodramas, stage entertainments popular with working-class audiences, often involved harsh landlords and the seduction of young women. In Western literary works melodrama is evident in the work of Charles Dickens, where reversals of fortune reflect social insecurity, and in the work of European writers such as Hugo, Balzac and Dostoevsky. Here, larger political and economic changes affecting the structure of society under rapid industrialisation affect the lives of the least articulate and least powerful in society.

In recent years, with the development of feminism, more serious attention has been given to the genre. Privileging women's experience, emotions and activities, melodramas have attracted critical attention as sources for portraying ideological conflict. Instead of dealing with political ideas at a polemical level, melodrama demonstrates social contradiction and ideological conflict in an accessible dramatic form, and presents problems at a personal level (see Elsaesser 1973). There are some claims that melodrama seeks to present things not as they are but as they ought to be, and looks not to the future but to a rose-tinted past (see, for example, Gledhill 1987). In Fifth Generation films, the 'search-for-roots' literature that preceded the films may indeed have had this motivation, but on the whole the past is held up for critical examination or provides a far more useful 'cover' as metaphor for present oppressions. The main areas for criticism are the repression of sexual desire and social injustices or the taboos and proscriptions surrounding feudal practices such as enforced marriage.

Melodrama thus points up the gap between ideological constructs and the context in which it operates; Fifth Generation films show how both Confucianism and the ideology of Mao's brand of socialism were inadequate for achieving social harmony, and depict the price paid for conforming to ideology in terms of human suffering. In these films the villain is most typically a patriarchal despot within a feudal system representing an unpredictable and hostile government. How far melodrama may merely reflect social change and how far it has a subversive role to play is much debated, as is the function of melodrama for its audiences. Douglas Sirk's melodramas of the 1950s operated as 'safety valves' for capitalism since they represented larger social conflicts in terms of the personal. Simply having problems represented relieved what might otherwise have been a feeling of powerlessness at being caught up in the operation of powerful and inhumane forces. It may be that the realistic representation of surface appearance, rather than the melodramatic form, served the purpose described – as a kind of outlet or expression for areas felt to be neglected by available representations. The same combination of melodramatic mode and contextualised realism is a feature of the Fifth Generation films.

The psychological function of narrative as 'correcting' unhappy life experiences is one attraction of the films for audiences: 'The resisting elements of the women's films lie in their positioning a female desire, a female subjectivity as theoretically possible, even if it cannot be achieved within existing frameworks' (Kaplan 1993: 13). In looking at how melodrama focuses on the problems of individuals within established social structures, and identifying moral polarities, however, there may be some implied pre-scription for social change. Furthermore, melodramatic output coincides with periods of intense social and ideological crises and appears to func-tion 'either subversively or as escapism' (Elsaesser 1973: 280).

An earlier tendency to combine realism with melodrama in Chinese film was notable when left-wing infiltrators into Shanghai film production after 1930 laid the foundations of a cinema that was both national and popular. Here, there was a strong concern for the realistic depiction of both peas-ants and the urban poor, though often within melodramatic plot structures. Chinese culture accepts the fusion of political discourse with social prac-tices which characterises melodrama, and intensifies points of conflict. This tradition was usefully adapted in films in the 1950s and 1960s to pro-mote the policies of the Chinese Communist Party. The analysis of *Yellow Earth*, below, shows how the melodramatic tradition is transformed by Fifth Generation director Chen Kaige to produce the new style of film-making.

Chinese film-makers have often used gender relations to represent class relations metonymically in their film practice. Those with leftist leanings, especially, 'often adopted the gender/class paradigm to signify the pat-terns of domination and exploitation that exist within the traditional family and social system' (Ma 1989: 103). The newly emerging socio-economic order was expressed in Chinese family drama as conflict between tradition and modernisation. Typically, as the next chapter will show, Confucianism was an ethical system regularly at odds with the political demands of Communism.

Case study: Yellow Earth

In 1939, during a temporary lull in the civil war between Communists and Nationalists, a young soldier arrives at a remote village north of the Yellow River. The soldier, Gu Ching, has a roving commission to collect folk songs to be used for propaganda purposes by the Red Army, based in the south at Yan'an. The village is famous for its songs. His arrival coincides with a wedding celebration, the adolescent bride carried, according to custom, in a palanquin to her middle-aged groom. The village is so poor that the fish traditionally served at the alfresco wedding banquet are wooden replicas. Billeted by request on the poorest family, a prematurely-aged widower and his 13-year-old daughter Cuiqiao and mute son Hanhan, Gu Ching sets about winning their confidence by helping out with domestic and farming tasks. He also extols the benefits of Communism at opportune moments during the working day. Although the old man is steeped in resignation to fate, and the boy too backward to understand, the daughter is fascinated to hear of the apparent equalities of men and women under Communism, and the abolition of enforced marriage. When Gu Ching leaves he promises to apply on Cuiqiao's behalf for a place in the army. However, Cuiqiao's prearranged wedding takes place in his absence and she subsequently tries to escape by crossing the river. On his return Gu Ching finds father and son engaged in a whole-village ceremony of prayer to the rain god. It is impossible to reach them because of the thronging crowd. Cuiqiao has apparently drowned whilst trying to reach the army in the south.

On its initial release *Yellow Earth* won four international awards, which helped to attract a curious home audience. It was recognised as the 'landmark' film of the Chinese avant-garde, seeming to invent a new kind of Chinese film language that had not been seen before but which was universally recognised as essentially filmic. The opening shot of the windswept Loess Plateau – the 'Yellow Earth' of the title – the lingering shots of the iconic Yellow River and the haunting folk melodies signal the examination of culture itself. This is a region resonant with meaning for the Chinese – believed to be the cradle of the Chinese nation with its river a metaphor for life and sustenance. Seen from an ironic perspective, of course, its

FIGURE 5 *Yellow Earth*

turbulent waters also carry away the topsoil and do little to irrigate the barren landscape. In fact, disastrous floods and sudden changes of course have been so frequent in the past that the river is known as 'China's Sorrow'.

As film critic Tony Rayns notes, every shot in this film carries 'a dazzling array of associations, connotations and implications' (Rayns 1986: 295). Added to the hardships imposed by the landscape are the father's reiteration of 'Fate' as the cause of suffering, and the superstitious rites which signal an attachment to old customs that will be hard to break; the final shots suggest the landscape itself, symbolising Chinese tradition, will engulf and destroy those who try to escape.

Further resonances were struck for the audience by some resemblance in the narrative to a work by popular director Xie Jin, *The Red Detachment of Women* (1961), in which a young peasant girl responds to a young soldier's influence and reinvents herself as a model soldier. At first sight *Yellow Earth* promises to be one more film in the 'model hero' mould, as the attractive Gu Ching combines a scholarly awareness with practical skill at darning his own socks, plus the strength to guide an ox-drawn plough. Ironically, his role is more sinister: he has raised impossible-to-fulfil hopes in Cuiqiao and won the affection of the later-abandoned Hanhan, her brother.

Having thus dispelled the myth of Party enlightenment brought to transform the lot of previously backward peasants, the film also attacks the cherished myth of instant rapport between the people and the Party. Gu Ching is as surprised at the unresponsiveness of the father to his message as the peasant is at the young man's naïvete. It is, however, the use of ritual dance that suggests most clearly that there is no solution to problems to be found in clinging to answers offered by authorities, whether the traditional power of the Dragon King to bring rain or the new political leader, Mao, to bring salvation. These rituals are presented as dances – the energetic drum-dance at the army camp when Gu Ching returns, with its frenzied hurling of limbs and red sashes, contrasted with the chaotic movements and chanting of the grass-garlanded villagers in the final scene. The initial impression of the drum-dance, which forms part of a ceremony to send off recruits to fight against the Japanese, may indeed be impressive but it is still a ritual, and therefore implicated as a force for oppression rather than liberation. Here the use of film language – and the inevitable parallels drawn – gives meaning to the combination of dances which is not present in the separate sequences.

Silence, music, and speech are all used to suggestive effect in the film. As Cuiqiao waits for her aged groom on the wedding night, silence reigns except for the girl's frightened breathing, heightening the sense of terror, particularly as an earlier scene has given a 'preview' of what to expect – an unattractive man of at least middle age. The presence of a dark hand pulling at the veil effectively conveys the horror of Cuiqiao's violation. Sudden silence is used to good effect in two previous scenes. As Cuiqiao attempts her escape across the Yellow River she sings the revolutionary song Gu Ching taught her; it is suddenly cut off in mid-phrase. This suggests a number of possibilities, apart from the most immediate one, that the boat has been overturned in the fast-flowing water. Amongst these is the idea that the promises of the song itself are meaningless. Earlier, sudden silence is also used to heighten drama and signal reversal of fortune when Cuiqiao enters her home to find the future in-laws waiting for her. At one moment she is smiling and almost bounding down the mountain with her burden of water pails, to a musical accompaniment of swelling strings on the soundtrack, then the music ceases abruptly as a close-up of her face shows the shock of recognition. The marriage will take place before Gu Ching returns.

The characterisation of soldier and peasants exploits the contrast between speech and silence. Gu Ching's eloquent polemics are contrasted with the monosyllabic responses of his host. He is surprised by the taciturnity of the wedding guests at the feast. Later, the father denies the need for singing when he is neither sad nor happy. Here a double polarity is thrown up. Gu Ching's words are empty because, as later events reveal, they do not mirror what actually happens. Yet a more important reason for distrusting speech is the purposes to which it can be put. Gu Ching is to collect the songs, he says, so the army 'can fit new words to them'. Winning the confidence of the peasants was one of Mao's explicit purposes on his 'Long March' through China. The spontaneity of the songs' origins are to become twisted for purposes of propaganda, as the peoples' allegiances are to be turned from their belief in the old gods to Mao and Communism.

The consequences of the spread of authoritarian teachings are also signalled in the early wedding scene when Cuiqiao, an anxious spectator to a ceremony which foreshadows her own, is framed in the doorway.

FIGURE 6 *Yellow Earth*

Immediately behind her are the characters of the four virtues and three obediences prescribed by Confucius for women. The shot clearly signals the girl's entrapment within a cruel system, without the need for dialogue. That the licence for gender oppression within the larger oppressions of poverty and the lack of power for women originates in the transcribed words of patriarchy is a message delivered entirely by the visual image. It is left for the audience to make the connections between these prescriptions and Mao's teachings on the role of women.

Landscape and colour are further features of the distinctive style which characterise this and other Fifth Generation films. The screen often resembles Chinese paintings not only in the frequent shots of landscape with a horizon not visible or very near the top of the screen, but also in the restricted colour scheme. The positioning of figures in the landscape suggests the interdependence of people and natural elements, as in the paintings. The restricted colour scheme underlines the unmitigated drabness of subsistence farming in this region, and allows the colour red to be used with extra vivid effect against the ochre and black which so often fill the frame. When the bridal palanquin's colour and the curtained nuptial chamber are echoed by the colour of Cuiqiao's padded jacket it is not only a somewhat unsubtle hint that a similar fate awaits her, but allows us to make the link, in the last scene, between the upturned floating jar and her drowning, in case we were in any doubt about the meaning of the sudden cessation of the song as the escape boat disappeared in the turbulence of the Yellow River. The floating jar's association with the girl and her daily task of water-carrying is made unmistakable by the floating crimson tether attached to it. There is also, of course, an ironic overturn of the usual associations of the colour itself in Chinese culture. Instead of happiness and life, it signals frustration and death.

The employment of ambiguity, symbol and metaphor, although potentially alienating to some of the audience, probably saved it from the extensive cuts and re-shooting necessary before the release of the more explicit *One and Eight*, directed by fellow graduate Zhang Junzhao, in the same year. Scenes where interpretation is left open provided protection for the film from a censorship board which was not versed in the subtleties of image interpretation. It was not uncommon for films to be withdrawn from circulation only after film critics detected an interpretation that escaped the censor.

At the same time, the film documents in minute detail the lives of the peasants and makes the characters memorable as individuals. The small acts of kindness which the family show to one another are recorded, as when the daughter makes shoes for the father – he accepts them whilst acknowledging half-apologetically to the soldier that he does not need them – or when the father gives part of his scanty luncheon gruel to his son. The film makes clear that the cause of their suffering is outside the family. The father's insistence on his daughter's marriage is not simply cruel – he needs the money paid for Cuiqiao to finance his son's future wedding and to pay off his dead wife's funeral costs. He seems as much bewildered as the others to find that doing his duty and finding husbands for his daughters as ordained by tradition does not end in happiness. Indeed, his older daughter has suffered poverty and physical abuse in her arranged marriage.

Although the film would seem to emphasise hardship as the province of the female – the point-of-view is often that of Cuiqiao and the theme of the songs is women's suffering – this should not be interpreted in the narrowest sense. The woman in Chinese cinema is often a metonym for the wider oppressions of feudalism. She suffers most because she is at the bottom of society's heap, but her suffering is just one of the many examples of the results of a general ignorance and hardship.

4   CONFUCIUS AND PATRIARCHY

Born in Lu, a small state in Shandong province, Confucius (551–479 BC) was China's first moral philosopher. He believed moral order and harmony were linked to traditional roles and structures: an ideal world was one of hierarchies where conventions governed actions. Acts directed towards ancestors were as important as those towards living men, and filial piety was the supreme virtue because he saw the family as a model for society at large. After his death, temples were set up for Confucian worship and his teachings became an essential part of the imperial examination system by which men entered the governing class. These examinations were officially abolished in 1905, but Confucian values continue to exert a profound influence on Chinese society.

Much of the teachings emphasised the role of the ruler, whose legitimacy depended on an inextricable mixture of his own virtue and the treatment of his subjects. He must be virtuous himself before transforming people and was obliged to operate in humane fashion, otherwise the mandate of heaven, or right to rule, could be lost and the subjects gain the right to rebel. In fact, rulers rarely behaved according to precepts, but the Confucian doctrine of loyalty and the benefits of office usually kept the chain of command unbroken.

For the purposes of government it clearly suited rulers to have huge numbers of administrators, scattered over a vast territory, adhering to doctrines that enjoined loyalty to superiors as a major virtue. Power was to be exercised by those who had been educated to use it, and a Confucian education became the main pathway to power in Chinese government. Entry to the administrative class implied access to texts and tutors that were beyond the means of most families, so that it was estimated that less than two per cent of the Chinese population belonged to families of Confucian degree holders (see Stacey 1983). Once elevated to the administrative ranks it was not in the interests of the 'mandarins', as the scholars were called, to rock the boat. As William Callahan writes, 'Confucianism did certainly support the mandarinate – that is why the mandarins supported Confucianism' (Callahan 1993: 71).

The family occupies a central position in Confucian culture, with filial piety, defined as lifelong service to parents, as its key virtue. This embraced loyalty and obligation to past generations: the family was a microcosm of society and operated under the same hierarchical system, with the most important relationship within the family being that between father and son. The male head of the family decided everything and his aim and duty was to maintain an unbroken lineage.

Developments in Confucian thought restricted the sphere of women. A woman's duty was to identify with her husband's welfare, show no bias or jealousy of concubines or their children, and refrain from remarrying after her husband's death. In the Confucian ideal family, individuals were to have no choice in choosing a spouse, but marriage was regarded as a transaction initiated by the groom's family whereby women were transferred from the ownership of her parents to the ownership of the husband. The wedding ritual was designed to impress upon the bride her subservience to her husband and his family, thus there was much use of bowing and veils. The bride would return to visit her own parents after three days, where distance permitted.

There were almost no grounds for divorce on the part of women, and severe restrictions existed regarding the marriage of widows. Great value was placed on wifely fidelity and children were the property of the husband's family. Women were not seen as members of either the natal or the marital family, and were officially subject to three obediences – to father, husband, and any future son they were to produce. They had a duty of fidelity to patrilineage, and temptations were removed as far as possible – there was segregation at an early age, and then domestic seclusion. Although chastity was the greatest virtue for a woman, women were the sexual prey of men in the husband's household. Wife and daughter-in-law beating was common and in fact enjoined in cases of disobedience, and suicide was the only escape for a woman in an intolerable situation. Such was the regularity of this form of release that it became a common literary motif.

Confucianism was widespread mainly because it suited existing beliefs and because, as Judith Stacey writes, 'many Confucian virtues were elite elaborations of widespread peasant attitudes' (Stacey 1983: 59). Apart from the intense study of texts required by examination candidates, educational materials other than examination texts were available for dissemination to the rest of the population. To encourage observance and initiate young people, texts used as popular primers in schools contained stories of extreme devotion to parents and were used to teach children over generations. Traditional Chinese law was based on Confucian teachings and upheld hierarchical distinctions such as the power of the husband over family and wife, including the right to chastise to death. In fact, the Confucian ideal of harmony was achieved by few. The wife had strong reasons for wishing to establish an independent conjugal household and the husband's family were at pains to make sure this did not happen.

The first wave of anti-Confucianism occurred in 1916–20, when radical liberals returning from Europe blamed Confucianism for China's failures: weakness before colonial powers and its inability to modernise. Later, Mao Zedong identified Confucianism as the ideology of the exploitative class; further, that it was responsible for a deep conservatism that made the Chinese closed to Western ideas. Despite the opposition to organised religion in Communist doctrine, apart from the overriding observance of Confucian values, for the vast majority of Chinese people religion continues to dominate much of social discourse, consisting of what Lynn Pan calls a 'rich jumble' to which three schools of thought contributed: Confucianism, Daoism and Buddhism (Pan 1987: 228). As a belief system,

Confucianism, despite its emphasis on the dead, lacked the mystical or supernatural element of religion, but did not directly conflict with popular Daoist and Buddhist belief systems that have extended into modern times.

A woman's place

The history of women in Chinese society can be generally divided into two eras – the 2,000 years of largely unchallenged Confucian family structure up to 1949, and the situation for women under Communist rule. The earlier period is usually described as 'traditional' as distinct from the more recent 'modern' era. However, for reasons that will be made clear, they more often represent differences in concept than actuality.

There was a variety of marriage in traditional society according to the economic circumstances of the local community. There were also differences between rich and poor, urban and rural practices: it was not uncommon, for instance, for women in elite families to be educated. Whereas women of wealthy families were more often confined to the home, and even urban women of elite families would meet only household servants, peasant women were more likely to have access to the company of other females through activities such as water-carrying or land-work. Women and young children were more economically important in a peasant family, not only for domestic but field labour. The fact that peasants frequently went into debt to afford proper rituals provides evidence of the struggle to conform to the elite ideal.

Historically, the legacy of Confucian ethics for centuries restricted the role of women to the domestic sphere and to their position at the bottom of the hierarchy of authority within the family (although status might be changed to one of relative power as the mother of a male heir and later mother-in-law). The family was 'hierarchical, authoritarian, and patrilineal, embodying a strict sexual and generational division of labour' (Andors 1983: 12). The continuance of patrilocal practice, whereby the female 'married out' of her own family and went to live with her husband's household perpetuated her role as 'outsider' until a male heir was produced for the new family. The birth of a girl was generally regarded as a disaster, as she would leave the family on marriage and have to be provided with a dowry. The disappointment at the birth of a female was occasionally reflected in the name she was given, and infanticide of females was frequent enough to be reflected in population statistics. Wealthy families sometimes adopted out 'excess' girls to avoid the expense of feeding and dowering them.

Despite birth control campaigns, the difficulties of obtaining contraceptive supplies of a reliable kind led to failure in this area and late marriage was recommended as a more effective method for restricting growth of numbers. Later, the one-child policy adopted in an attempt to prevent population growth makes the female a further focus of problems, and in fact has led to the 'disappearance' of thousands of female children as the 'official' register of births by gender has become distorted compared with the ratio of males-to-females previously recorded. The problem of the disappearing females highlights the continuance of the traditional view of the undesirability of female offspring (see Croll 1995).

Child betrothal was a common practice and the potential bride would be transferred to the receiving family at an early age, having the advantage of releasing her own family from the expense of feeding her and relieving the potential mother-in-law of some household chores. Missionary accounts of females sold into slavery in Yan'an Province as late as 1935 said it was 'not untypical' when one girl was sold by her opium-addicted father (Jaschok & Miers 1994: 195). Concubinage, whereby a married man would take additional females into the household for sexual purposes, was common among elite families. Whether for purposes of displaying wealth, ensuring family continuance or for other reasons, it led to inheritance disputes and 'much scheming for favour among the various mothers and their sons' (Ebrey 1991: 39).

However, it was the practice of footbinding that was the most infamous cruelty inflicted by Confucian men, and was widespread across classes into the late-nineteenth century. Better marriage prospects seem the most likely reason for the practice of footbinding for women who were also needed for field work. This custom began to be prevalent in the tenth century, as an erotic practice amongst the elite classes, and spread throughout China. It was responsible for a deterioration in women's health and persisted as late as the 1940s, when there was a campaign for its abolition in the Yan'an area, although it had been declared illegal in 1902. Even peasant families believed that women with small feet would be more attractive to men and there were reports of women working in fields on their knees because walking was so difficult for them. It was first attacked as a practice in the mid-nineteenth century, for nationalist reasons, after the humiliating defeats of the Opium Wars. Ironically, Nationalists blamed physical weakness in males on the poor health of physically inactive mothers.

Early reform movements were unsuccessful because, as Kay Johnson reports 'Chinese women were embedded in perhaps the oldest, most highly developed, male-dominated kinship system in history' (Johnson 1983: 24). In 1919 a democratic surge of opinion known as the May Fourth movement called for schools to be opened for women but their aims were generally not realised – it was mainly a student movement not relevant to countrywomen. One of China's foremost modern writers, Lu Xun (1881–1936), attacked Confucianism at this period in his short story called 'Diary of a Madman' (1918), the first book to be written in vernacular Chinese. However, the May Fourth movement met with opposition from the Nationalist government and in 1927 Chiang Kai-shek decided to eliminate Communist competition and suppress all unions, including those for women.

A minority of women enjoyed better opportunities beyond the Confucian guidelines. Some women in elite families were educated and there were opportunities developing at the turn of century in urban areas and in the textile factories of the Pearl River Delta. The introduction in 1950 of the new Marriage Law was an index of the importance the Communist government attached to changing women's position in society. Local Party cadres, however, whose task it was to oversee the implementation of the provisions, were reluctant to act against tradition and offend the people on whose support they depended.

Before the Long March, when Mao and his supporters were in Jianxi Province, strenuous physical exercise and military training for both men and women were encouraged, and images of Jianxi women presented an alternative to traditional expectations and underlined the 'duties, responsibilities and possibilities of contemporary Chinese women under Communism' (Hong 1997: 175). Chi Pen's collection of testimonial essays and photographs of smiling women workers also provide persuasive evidence of the desirability of new active roles. In the introduction he writes of how 'enjoying the right to work in every field, they eagerly "hold up half the sky"' (Chi 1977: 5).

In fact, the Communist government distanced itself from the Women's movement and said that women's liberation would follow as a result of changes in the whole economic system, with women as potential workers and potential soldiers. At the same time the Communists realised that peasants' attitudes to women would not change overnight. The Party had to be careful to keep a balance between 'women's demands and men's prejudices' (Hong 1997: 163). In fact the anti-Lin Biao and Confucius campaign in 1973 demonstrated the relative ineffectiveness of legislation in the face of tradition, and Hong even goes so far as to claim that 'in the 1990s inequality between men and women [was] actually increasing' (Hong 1997: 303). In rural areas women are sent back home in times of unemployment, with female unemployment rising as result of technological reform; in cities women are laid off while men retain jobs. Furthermore, there is unequal pay and it is harder for female graduates to find jobs. There has been some reappearance of the concubinage and prostitution that the CCP tried to stamp out. Marxism is perhaps as much to blame as Confucianism for the failure of modern Chinese women to gain equality, and as Hong suggests, Chinese women may never achieve full equality 'without challenging the simplistic reductionism of Marxism itself' (Hong 1997: 304)

Women in films

In the earliest Chinese films women were seen as victimised by patriarchal society yet were celebrated where they demonstrated the Confucian virtues of tolerance, patience and understanding. In *The Difficult Couple* (1913) the arranged marriage system was depicted, with the virtuous wife triumphing in the end by turning a blind eye to her husband's peccadilloes. In *Cheng the Fruit Seller* (1922), however, a dutiful daughter steps outside strict traditional boundaries to display herself to the eponymous tradesman and marries happily in the end. In these and many other films of the period, the accepted family structure gave the man the freedom to have several concubines, but the woman must remain chaste. Prostitutes were the alternative form of female portrayal, so the two images of femininity, the wife and the courtesan, have appeared consistently on the Chinese screen.

In the 1930s, contrasting with the Confucian construction of the female, a type of bourgeois femininity emerged, especially in films set in Shanghai. Most of these films typically depicted women enjoying a Western lifestyle which included night clubs with jazz bands, cocktails and elegant fashions. In many ways similar to the portrayal of 'party' girls in the films of Weimar Germany of the late 1920s and early 1930s, the decadence was condemned by the punishment of the woman, whether by death or social censure, whilst at the same time she was displayed for the voyeuristic pleasure of the audience.

The 1930s also saw the emergence of the career woman, but such representations were likewise associated with unhappy outcomes. Only in the films made by leftist directors, whose films prefered the 'asexual revolutionary woman' motivated by political idealism, was there any positive outcome to the women's actions. This image was carried to an extreme in the Cultural Revolution when sexuality was excluded from the portrayal of virtually all women on film. By contrast, a number of films made in the late 1940s presented a more complex type of femininity. In *Long Love the Mistress* (1947) and *Spring in a Small Town* (1948), the protagonists presented both sexual awareness and resourcefulness in dealing with traditional family situations. However, it was clear that these attributes were to be deployed within the patriarchal family situation, and to be accounted successful only because they did not disturb it. Contrasting with the weak males who partner them, they were early prototypes of the characters that have since dominated Zhang Yimou's films.

The post-1949 representation of women in films was dictated by Party requirements to show women as model builders of socialism, embracing Communist Party doctrines in various 'liberated' social roles and willingly accepting or ignoring the fact that the imposition of such an order necessitated their oppression and submission. Family groups graced by these revolutionary heroines inevitably reaped material rewards. Later, in the 1960s and 1970s, women were more strongly politicised and even militarised, seeming at times robot-like and superhuman in their achievements. However, the new questioning and assertion of a 'modern' view of film aesthetics in the late 1970s at the end of the ten years of the Cultural Revolution, together with an interest in documentary, led to a rejection of the more theatrical aspects of film representation and a trend to greater realism in terms of psychological normality in character depiction.

After the graduation of the Fifth Generation film-makers, screen characters became more realistic both in their situations and range of choices. In particular, contradiction and ambiguity of response gave a sense of complexity and depth to female characters. Women in 1980s films were thus reassessed as subject to repressive forces beyond their control rather than victims of their own tendency to self-denial and sacrifice, as in pre-1949 representations. These films depicted a wide range of women's experiences and sufferings during the Cultural Revolution.

New wave Chinese films take as a main theme the conflict between sexual fulfilment and the demands of the state. Kaplan (1991) points out that the entire focus of the film *Army Nurse* (1985), for instance, is the conflict between love and duty. She argues that films by female directors are often about the impossibility of a mutual desire, whilst male directors are concerned with fantasies of seduction or revenge on women for men's cultural repression and passive position. A seduction scene can often be read as male fantasy of female desire, always wanting arousal and happy to be satisfied, or as essentially (from the feminist point of view) a rape scene. Kaplan further points out that the new machismo apparent in the men, as in the rape scene in *Red Sorghum*, is a cause for concern, suggesting it is a revenge fantasy for the new-found liberation in the Communist state which insists on parity between the sexes in the public sphere.

However, though some critics argue that if modern Chinese women suffer from being reduced to a 'signifier in a patriarchal sign system' (Widmer & Wang 1993: 8), modern Chinese men seem no better off. The gaze of frustrated desire is more often mutual in Chinese films, and the entire signifying of sexual relations may stand as a metaphor for the broader polit-ical, social and intellectual frustration of both genders. In fact, Chinese men may be more psychically damaged than women in their submission to the State. In *Red Sorghum* a perfect male virility construct, which includes sexual, economic and patriotic success, provides narcissistic pleasures for Chinese men; the film's representation of its anarchic peasant hero may respond in a profound way to the audience's needs, and thus account for its popularity.

In the 1980s a period of introspection and interest in film aesthetics gave rise to more 'psychologised' heroines. Women now have 'high signify-ing values' (Yau 1989: 11) as objects of narrative change as well as for the formal structuring of the voyeuristic gaze. The question of how far Chinese films of the 1980s show a progression of representation in feminist terms is problematic. Laura Mulvey asserted that men unconsciously structured film form to suit their own 'gaze', and in so doing established the psycho-analytic framework for feminist film studies (Mulvey 1975). In this scenario, the gaze of the onlooker is constructed as male and the woman becomes a spectacle for his pleasure. Women in Chinese films of the 1980s are fre-quently presented as sexualised beings, and, as discussed in earlier chap-ters, attracted the displeasure of censors who accused Fifth Generation directors of pandering to Western tastes.

Children in 1980s films are often a source of conflict, either because they are, or might be, of the wrong (that is, female) gender, or used as weapons in the struggle for female power. They may increase the vulnerability of the family, or be positively lethal, as in *Ju Dou*, discussed in the final sec-tion of this chapter. The vengeful child in *Ju Dou* strikes a chord with those whose children were encouraged to denounce them during the Cultural Revolution.

Because for many new wave Chinese films marriage is a problematic institution which represents the imbalance of power in the wider society, there are few happy unions. Critics have remarked on the frequent pres-ence in Zhang Yimou's films of a hostile patriarchal figure who has absolute power and control over a wife he has 'bought' from her family and whom he torments. Parallel situations are presented in *Red Sorghum*, where the heroine is married to a leper who is never glimpsed, apart from his hand stretching towards the bridal bed, and *Raise the Red Lantern*, where four concubines are forced to take part in a humiliating nightly ritual where they wait to hear which of them the husband has chosen to sleep with – a choice which carries with it other favours such as foot massage and the right to choose the daily dinner menu. In these and other films the husband may be seen as representing the arbitrary and divisive power of the State.

Tales of female sexual transgression and physical punishment were dramatised in many mainland films of the 1980s. In *The Corner Forsaken by Love* (1981), a village girl who has sex with her lover before marriage commits suicide after her lover is arrested and imprisoned for the transgressive act. In *Bloody Morning* (1990) another village woman goes insane and commits suicide on the wedding night after her husband discovers she is not a virgin. However, since the early 1980s some tolerance and understanding of the woman's situation has been shown, as in *A Girl from Hunan* (1986) when a girl married to an infant husband transgresses and gives birth to a boy but is allowed to stay in the family.

The influence of Hong Kong cinema's sensuous females such as the heroine of Stanley Kwan's *Rouge* (1987) was also visible in mainland productions of the 1990s, such as *Yesterday's Wine* (1995). Nevertheless, it is certainly evident that 'women remain the object of attraction, obsession, and sometimes scandal in various kinds of films by male directors' (Zhang & Xiao 1998: 284).

A Chinese film star

Gong Li is famous in China and worldwide art-house cinemas for her portrayals of 'indomitable heroines willing to challenge China's prevailing gerontology and sexual mores' (Goldman 1993: 8). Her personal life has become the staple of tabloid magazine gossip in her homeland and fuelled a cult amongst Chinese women who admire the way she combines a liberated lifestyle, as embodied in the glamorous image of an internationally renowned film star, with more traditional routines, such as making a 'dutiful' marriage and working hard.

Gong was born in Shenyang, northern China, in 1965, the youngest of five children. Her parents were university teachers, which meant, Gong says, that the whole family had a tough time during the Cultural Revolution and afterwards, when the middle class were stripped of privileges and property in China under Mao (Weidmann 1996: 48). Frustrated in her first career choice as a singer, Gong enrolled in the Central Academy of Drama's acting department in 1985 (her application had been turned down several times) and graduated in 1989.

Gong Li is physically striking, taller than the average Chinese, with a fluid grace of movement acquired from dance training as a child. James Dalrymple comments on the proliferation of magazine pictures of Gong Li, replacing those of Chairman Mao as a cultural icon and signifying the promise of 'thrilling things' that have been hidden and repressed for centuries (Dalrymple 1995: 16).

While still a 21-year-old student she was 'discovered' by Fifth Generation director Zhang Yimou, who secretly observed her in rehearsal, an event which seems to prefigure the infamous scene in *Ju Dou* where Gong, playing the eponymous heroine, attracts voyeuristic attention whilst washing her body. Zhang cast her in *Red Sorghum*, his directorial debut. Gong went on to star in six more films of his after *Red Sorghum*, as 'Dietrich to his von Sternberg' (Wilkinson 2000: 36).

Her portrayal of the headstrong owner of a winery in *Red Sorghum* was a breakthrough in terms of the representation of women in Chinese films. She plays a peasant's daughter, initially sold into marriage, who takes control after her husband's death and subsequently enjoys a sexual relationship with a virile peasant, before being killed by Japanese in the sorghum fields of the film's title. In the early sexual encounters she combines outward submissiveness to events beyond her control with an underlying strength of purpose and is a commanding presence when she directs operations in the winery. In the film the camera favours her point of view, 'according her a voice in a society in which women are frequently denied one' (Wilkinson 2000: 37). The film is also significant for the lengths it goes to display Gong as an object of desire. Shrouded in red and encased in a sedan, Zhang's camera lingers on her features, in part projecting the desires of her carriers, in particular, her future rapist/husband, but also for audience consumption. The film ran for two years in Chinese cinemas and achieved cult status amongst Chinese youths; songs from the soundtrack were sung during the Tiananmen student demonstrations in June 1989.

Gong's second film, also directed by Zhang Yimou, was a commercial thriller, *Codename Cougar* (1989), in which she brought added glamour to an otherwise routine, but competently made, film about a plane hi-jacking.

In *The Terracotta Warrior* (1990), Gong played opposite Zhang Yimou in a romance located at the beginning in the Qin dynasty (c. 200 BC). It was a lavish and lively production, with a plot which combines love story, stunts and comedy: the warrior Mong, played by Zhang Yimou falls in love with court handmaiden, Twon, played by Gong Li. When their love affair is discovered, she walks into a wall of flame and he is encased as a Terracotta warrior and buried with thousands of others in the tomb of the First Emperor of China at Xi'an. In the 1920s Twon is reincarnated as a tour guide whose plane crashes into the Emperor's tomb. Mong comes back to life, the pair are reunited and comedy ensues as Mong tries to cope with modern life, equipped only with the weapons and knowledge of the Qin dynasty.

Gong went on to specialise in roles where oppressed women take control, albeit with varying success, in a series of films directed by Zhang. Her relationship with the already-married Zhang fuelled both media gossip and official Party disapproval. *Ju Dou*, in which she played the wife of a sadistic mill-owner, is treated in more detail below. In *Raise the Red Lantern* her character is again forced into marriage, this time becoming the fourth wife of the head of a traditional family who is keen to father a son. His usual evening routine is to make his wives wait at the threshold of their separate apartments within the remotely situated clan dwelling to see which of them he will sleep with that night. His chosen bedmate's apartment is duly decorated with brightly-lit red lanterns. The film was not so much a study of the relationship of the husband with his wives as an exploration of the consequences for the wives of such a relationship – jealousies beneath a veneer of politeness and clandestine affairs punishable by death lead to immense psychological strain and eventual madness. Gong portrayed the transition from headstrong student determined to hold her own in the bizarre household through the various stages of humiliation and eventual break-down, with unswerving credibility.

It was as a heavily pregnant peasant woman in *The Story of Qiu Ju*, almost unrecognisable under layers of padded clothing, that Gong further extended her range and proved her versatility. The film won her the Best Actress award at the Venice Film Festival and for the first time the whole-hearted approval of the Chinese authorities. Her previous films had incurred censure and censorship for the challenge they represented to the existing order, although apparently disguised as fables from past, pre-liberation days. *The Story of Qiu Ju* was taken as a tribute to the courage and indomi-tablilty of Chinese womanhood in its portrayal of a woman who will stop at nothing in her struggle for redress when her husband is injured by the village headman in a dispute over land use. Adapted from a short story, the film also apparently paid tribute to the new justice rules that had been introduced to modernise the operation of law in China. Gong prepared for the role by living among the peasants for months before shooting, study-ing their expressions and mannerisms. The deliberate movements and stiff-jawed, immobile face of the peasant woman are in keeping with the film's naturalistic cinematography. The variety of settings, in her progress from village to town to city and the encounters with masculine authority figures allowed Gong to demonstrate a range of understated emotions and the director to comment on some of the bizarre features of China's transition to modernity.

Gong played a glamorous prostitute-turned-wife in *Farewell My Concu-bine* (1993), directed by Chen Kaige. She took a supporting role as success-ful rival to Leslie Cheung for the affections of the leading man of a Peking Opera troupe. This film, which is perhaps the best known of all the New Wave Chinese films in the West, was banned in China until 1997.

In *Soul of a Painter* (1993), based on the life of a real artist, Gong also played an ex-prostitute who subsequently takes up a career as a painter. The joint venture film was five years in production. Costs were high – it was mostly shot in Paris – and investors were nervous, especially after the events of Tiananmen Square. The plot concerns a female artist in the 1920s, who causes a scandal by painting female nudes. After finding fame in Paris

FIGURE 7 *Farewell My Concubine*

she is employed as a Professor at Nanjing Art School. However, the local press attacks her work and personal reputation, causing her to return to Paris, where she eventually dies a lonely death. This twist reflects to some extent Gong's own view of the tabloid press, whom she has alternately avoided and condemned for the stories they wove around her own personal life. She has been generally hostile to the press and thinks that they should face harsh penalties for their distortions (see Morris 2000). Gong again extended her range dramatically, agreeing to be made-up to depict a 70-year-old woman.

Mary from Beijing (1993) was directed by celebrated Hong Kong director, Sylvia Chang. Gong here plays a woman whose lack of a residence card prevents her from finding a job in Hong Kong and who becomes mistress to a man who treats her with indifference. She finally leaves him, finds work as a tour guide and, in an up-beat ending – which is a rarity for Gong – finds hope in the renewal of a relationship with a divorced man.

It was in her next film, *To Live* (1994), that Gong Li deployed her acting range to excellent effect as the wife of a wastrel who reforms after he returns from a spell as an accidental conscript for the Peoples' Liberation Army. In the early part of the film, Gong's role is no more taxing than her previous roles in Zhang Yimou's films; that of the suffering and much put-upon wife. It is in her convincing and understated portrait of the ageing wife living under constant dread of the authorities, rather than in the reactions to her children's fates, that she is memorable. Gong went on to play in *The Great Conqueror's Concubine* (1994), a 'turgid historical epic' (Rayns 1994: 22), only to return to Zhang for their final collaboration to date, *Shanghai Triad* (1995). In the latter she reverts from the hard-bitten mistress who confiscates tips from a lowly nightclub hostess to the simple peasant girl she once was, although she again meets a tragic end.

In *Temptress Moon* (1996) Gong played the drug-addicted head of a wealthy traditional family who takes imperious charge of the household but who then falls prey to the machinations of a Shanghai-based gang of fraudsters when her lover, played by Leslie Cheung, is revealed as a gigolo who preys on wealthy women. However, as in *Farewell My Concubine* her role is subsumed into the requirements of the films larger themes, namely the decadence of colonial Shanghai and the interest of the relationships within the traditional household with its power-struggles and incestuous relationships.

In Chen Kaige's lavish production of *The Emperor and the Assassin* (1999), Gong plays a glamorous go-between. In one memorable scene the character she plays insists that her face be branded, to provide convincing cover for her double-agent role. It may be said that this scene encapsulates both Gong's strengths as an actress and her appeal to her audience – her suffering is not only stoically borne, but accepted as the price of success for her mission.

Gong had an English-speaking role opposite Jeremy Irons in *Chinese Box* (1997), directed by Wayne Wang. She was familiar with her part as an ex-nightclub-owner but her character was underdeveloped – the film did not do well at the box office. In her most recent role, *Breaking the Silence* (2000), she has more scope for her talents as the mother of a deaf child she is determined to help communicate. It is to be hoped that future films will allow her to add to the considerable range she has already demon-strated, and that she will be able to resist mere reprises, a possible result of enrolment into the star system spin-off resulting from heavily-financed joint productions.

For a Chinese audience Gong represents women who question their role in patriarchal structures and engage with the wider issue of gender relation-ships. The men who play opposite her are often seen as victims not only of her beauty but of her superior intelligence (although, as in *Shanghai Triad* (1995), this can also be reduced to a kind of low cunning or desper-ate bid for survival). Berenice Reynaud writes that Gong Li 'knows how to project a mask of pain' (Reynaud 1993: 13). She further suggests that Zhang Yimou has taken the opportunity to vicariously live his lost youth through the star/lover who is the same age as the student protesters of Tiananmen Square. There is no doubt that Gong Li's status as China's leading film actress contributed greatly to the success of Zhang Yimou's films.

On the other hand, part of her popularity with Chinese audiences can be ascribed to the more 'traditional' and conservative qualities she displays. According to publicity, when she is in need of advice she goes home to her mother in Shenyang. She claims to dislike portraying sex sirens (as in *Shanghai Triad*), does not watch Western films with female stars, and works practically every day. Indefatigable in her devotion to her career, she aver-ages three films a year, as well as working on television commercials and re-launching her career as a singer. Although officially tied to a Beijing job as a drama teacher and not allowed to leave the country without permission, she is very wealthy and has the freedom to come and go as she pleases.

In her preparatory study for the roles she plays, and the seriousness with which she approaches her work, as well as the weight her perform- ance lends the films she stars in, Gong has been compared to Hollywood actresses such as Meryl Streep. Even she sees herself as a working actress rather than a glamorous star. After the separation from Zhang Yimou in 1995, she was reported to be angry about the publicity. Zhang Yimou expressed his gratitude to Gong Li – he said they had made ten films in eight years together and hoped for more to follow. Gong was awarded a contract by L'Oreal Cosmetics to promote their products and, having proved her singing abilities in *Shanghai Triad*, she is recording an album of Mandarin songs. She will next been seen in Wong Kar-wai's provisionally titled *2047*, a film about the fiftieth anniversary of the British handover of Hong Kong to main- land China.

Case study: Ju Dou

Zhang Yimou's film about an adulterous relationship in a strictly traditional society is a powerful indictment of Confucian values and the way in which women are rendered powerless in situations of extreme repression.

Ju Dou, a university student in 1920s China, is sold in marriage to Jinshan, the elderly owner of a village dye-works. At night he takes a sadistic pleasure in torturing his wife in their loft-bedroom over the workshop and by day Ju Dou labours alongside the single male employee, Tianqing, who is also Jinshan's adopted nephew and lives on the premises. Every morning Ju Dou descends from the loft bedroom above the workplace and washes her bruised body, spied on by Tianqing through a crack in the wooden partition between the wash room and the stable. Believing Tianqing is sympathetic, she takes advantage of her husband's temporary absence to seduce him and eventually gives birth to a son, whom her husband apparently accepts as his own and who is named Tianbai by the family elders. Jinshan is crippled by a fall from his horse and then accidentally killed by falling into the dye-vat, watched by the laughing

FIGURE 8 *Ju Dou*

child. After performing an elaborate and exhausting burial ritual, the lovers are compelled by tradition, embodied in the family elders and village gossips, to live separately, enjoying only infrequent visits and secret love-making. Enraged by village gossip about his parentage, Tianbai drowns Tianqing in the dye-vat when he finds the ageing pair almost unconscious in the storage cellar. When she realises her lover's fate, Ju Dou sets fire to the works and perishes in the flames.

Interspersed with recurring long shots of the small town, where the tall racks of primary-coloured cloth stand above the rooftops, the love scenes are contrasted with the malicious cruelty of the husband and the sullen menace of the boy. The difficult family situation is aggravated by the family elders who have control over crucial aspects of the lives of the protagonists and by the hostile townsfolk, given to spying, sneering and gossip. The labyrinthian dye-works is enclosed and separate from the town, but its inhabitants are subject to its social mores and influence

Although Ju Dou may be said to be the instigator of the adulterous affair, it is only when Tianqing shows signs of wanting to intervene, and in an act with both literal and symbolic power plants an axe into the staircase leading up to the bedroom during one of the nightly beating sessions, that she takes advantage of her husband's temporary absence and seduces him. In a scene which shows her taking charge of the situation, and which angered censors, she deliberately turns when washing to show her naked body to the watching Tianqing. When her husband becomes paralysed, it seems as if she will be free to enjoy a pleasurable relationship with Tianqing, and the lovers are for a while able to savour revenge by forcing Jinshan to witness their happiness. However, the fear that she may be pregnant again, this time with no one willing to believe the paralysed Jinshan could be the father, leads Ju Dou to attempt painful folk remedies leading to a loss of fertility. Her husband's subsequent death leaves her alone with a son who hates her. Tianqing is forced to live elsewhere because although widowed Ju Dou cannot, according to tradition, remarry and it will offend propriety for the pair to live in the same house. Forced to endure a trial by mourning then a separation which is so painful the lovers contemplate suicide, Ju Dou's response to the murder of her lover is to destroy the family home.

Ju Dou's choices are severely constrained by the social situation. There is no option for her to merely obey and accept her destiny as Jinshan's wife, because the price, that of certain death, is too high. Ju Dou is a woman in an impossible position: having been sold into marriage she lacks even the possibility of a return to her widowed mother. If she does nothing and continues to obey her husband she will die – Jinshan has already beaten two former wives to death. However, an obstacle to rebellion is traditional Chinese society's attitude and the treatment of those who appear to flout the rules. The protagonists are aware that the death penalty will ensue if their relationship is revealed. They successfully complete the strenuous mourning ritual, which entails throwing themselves in front of the funeral procession for a prescribed number of times to demonstrate grief, but the ensuing separation and the enmity of local society is too much for them – they would rather risk death by suffocation in the dye cellar.

The nature of the gender imbalance of power is such that it over-rules the bonding of the lovers. Although Tianqing is a desirable and faithful lover, he is essentially bound by male loyalties, content at first to be a watcher, morally timid and afraid to break with traditional taboos. He is passive, preferring to hide and risk suffocation rather than attempt to escape with Ju Dou. In a sense he too can be seen as an oppressor, an aspect made explicit in a scene where he accuses Ju Dou of having poisoned her husband, his uncle, and strikes her. Here the patriarchal tie and the horror of being implicated in killing an older male relative overwhelms his relief that the husband is finally out of the way. The narrative presents a situation which would be familiar to a Chinese audience, despite the substantial changes introduced by the Marriage Laws in 1950 and its later revisions. However, it is also a critique of contemporary Chinese society. As discussed in Chapter 1, critique by allegory was a method familiar to the Chinese intellectual and in this case it is signalled early on by the anonymity of the setting where 'the nameless village points to a named nation' (Callahan 1993: 70).

Ju Dou and Tianqing fear gossip because Confucianism is imbued in social values: 'a tightly structured extended family in which one constantly runs up not against "God" but against other watching, listening human beings' (Chow 1991: 61). Tianbai ironically carries out the greatest Confucian crime, in killing both his 'fathers': having as a child observed the struggles of the drowning cripple, a chilling smile on his face, he deliberately throws a weakened Tianqing into the same dye-vat. Ju Dou's son becomes her new master under the Confucian order, having saved her as she tried to die in her lover's arms. Ju Dou's subsequent burning of the dye works can be seen as vain attempt to destroy ' the patriarchal space' (Callahan 1993: 67).

Amongst its other messages, the film shows how repressive regimes also work to create social identities. Ju Dou and Tianqing's constant air of watchfulness and fear is a result of oppression within the house where they both live and work and the awareness of the influence of a wider social system represented by the village people. Inside the house, the ancestral memorial board – ironically inscribed with the Confucian motto 'be benevolent and virtuous' – appears in six shots in the film: a reminder to the protagonists of their position within the Confucian value system. Ju Dou's struggle against her social placement as a woman in feudal China is thus a protest against Confucian values still operating in modern China, where the Communist regime is seen to have many of the attributes of the Confucian system, including a tyrannical hierarchical structure perpetuated by popular support. In the Chinese context, both Communism and Confucianism are patriarchal systems of domination: 'comm-fucian-ism' (Callahan 1993: 53). The repeated use of the long shot of the village with its drying racks showing above the other roofs further signals the timeless, unchanging nature of the village and its mores.

5 POST-SOCIALIST CONCERNS

The demonstrations that took place in Chinese cities from April to May 1989 were fuelled by dashed hopes. Rising expectations regarding civil and political rights combined with relative deprivation in social and economic standing to produce a sense of general discontent. The apparently spontaneous mass uprising that stemmed from student complaints gained the support of people from all social classes and occupations. The unequal distribution of new wealth was one source of complaint: pensioners, academics, and low- or fixed-earning workers had failed to benefit from Deng's reforms, and were further disadvantaged by inflation. The popular perception was that Party officials were getting benefits denied to the population at large. The fall in living standards brought with it the unfamiliar experience of unemployment, made worse by a lack of social security and social welfare benefits.

Although personal freedoms in China had increased – religious practice, for instance, was tolerated – social controls in place in China were as firm as always, and the Press was still under government control. The continued dependency on the *danwei*, or work unit, likewise remained a powerful means of social control. In China, a person's work unit is assigned at the end of the individual's education, and is unlikely to be changed. The work unit in turn assigns housing, travel permits and health insurance. A citizen also needs a residence permit and ration card, issued by the work unit. The Party Secretary in the unit even has power to determine such things as marriage and divorce.

Housing is usually attached to the work unit, and there are often dormitories for young singles or couples; females are more likely to live with their families. Mutual help is forthcoming from neighbours, as well as conflict management. Unit leaders' intervention in private matters is quite common. The use of dossiers or records kept of conduct and progress are a means of social control through most people's wish to keep a clean record, and civil rewards and penalties are a standard organisational method.

Technological development has made it easier to gain knowledge of personal freedoms enjoyed in Western societies and breeds aspirations. It is currently acceptable to have short-wave radio and listen to foreign broadcasts; foreign news magazines are available and television news has widened information. However, the fear of 'Western pollutants' such as materialism, depravity and crime discourages anything more than superficial contact with foreigners.

Developments in agriculture fuelled inflation. Agricultural policy had been reversed, and at the 1987 Party Congress it was announced that peasants could buy land they were working and pass it on as inheritance. Increased income was ascribed to the contract system, with workers allowed to sell extra produce and engage in sideline occupations. The dismantling of communes and the establishment of the contract system operating at household level had brought prosperity to many peasants, but low grain production was associated with hoarding and the ability to sell off at high prices, as well as the commercial attractiveness of other crops.

Internal migration was another source of concern. By 1982, up to 20 per cent of China's population lived in urban centres (see Goldstein & Goldstein 1992). Rural to urban migration was to be controlled as policy but is not so easy to implement. Coastal regions became flooded with workers willing to live in the shanty towns where they were then easily exploited. Housing shortages exacerbated migration problems. In April 1985 exiled youths returned to Beijing illegally in hundreds, claiming to speak for thousands who were still in the countryside under harsh conditions. They staged a sit-in on the steps of the CCP headquarters and sought legal permission to return to Beijing. The house waiting lists in Beijing were already several years long.

Measures introduced to limit population growth, although largely successful, have caused some hardship in cities and have been patchily enforced in the countryside, where some 75 per cent of the population still live. Now modernisers practise a stringent and sometimes cruel system of birth control, although strategies such as delayed marriage, free birth control equipment and abortions, and financial disincentives have helped to limit families. The policy has also produced other problems. There has been much pressure for women to have abortions when they conceive outside the plan for childbirth quotas, and since ultra-sound scanning was introduced in the late 1980s, it has been possible to detect the gender of the foetus. Many women succumbed more readily to pressure if the foetus proved to be female. Others may have practised female infanticide or concealed female births, as 'reported sex ratios for second and subsequent births are strongly skewed in favour of sons' (Ebrey 1999: 325).

Not least, the sheer physical and mental toll of the last fifty years of Chinese history has itself caused problems for the population as a whole. A study of how culture relates to health, based on patients of Hunan Medical College, demonstrated the links between symptoms and societal concerns (see Kleinman 1986). China's long history of natural disasters and wars caused suffering on a massive scale. Interviews revealed that people felt angry and betrayed by leaders, particularly Mao. Ex-Red Guards in particular were bitter because of education and career opportunities lost during the Cultural Revolution. The characteristics of the 'lost generation' stereotype, according to the study, are that they 'possess poor work habits, lack moral commitment, are disaffected and at times resort to illegal activities' (Kleinman 1986: 159).

A number of anti-government demonstrations were abandoned in early January 1987 because of police controls, and bitterness was created by the arrest of leaders, many of whom were subsequently expelled from the Party. Zhao Ziyang was elected in place of Hu Yaobang, who had been scapegoated for the student unrest. Veterans attacked 'spiritual pollution' in a series of articles and speeches against foreign influence and giving in to the demands of students to make life less monotonous. They hinted that the reform programme was responsible for China's problems.

Corrupt practices by Party officials were increasingly reported by the media, but a corruption case in Hainan in mid-1985, when business people appeared to be selling on cars all over China, was played down for fear of discrediting the whole of the Special Economic Zone concept. Dissent was apparent in the Seventh National People's Congress in 1988 and the foreign press were present to observe debates when Zhao called for cuts in bureaucracy, cutting off contracts and perks. However, by then the chief worry was inflation. Price liberalisation led to rapid rises, suppliers began hoarding and consumers rushed to buy. Inflation curbs became a matter of urgency and Zhao and Li Peng set about an urgent economic reform programme to combat rising prices. By the end of the summer panic buying was a regular occurrence in Shanghai and there began to be major pressure on banks. Consumerism was growing apace but so were inequalities. Under Mao the 'Four Musts' had been a bicycle, a radio, a watch and a sewing machine. In Deng Xiaoping's reforms they were replaced by the 'Eight Bigs' – a colour television, a refrigerator, a stereo, a camera, a motorcycle, a suite of furniture, a washing machine and an electric fan. The 'Three Highs' necessary to get a wife were: high salary, higher education and a height of over five feet six inches!

Until 1990 the majority of urban adults worked in state-owned enterprises and enjoyed an 'iron rice-bowl' of lifetime employment, egalitarian wages and welfare benefits. The 1980s introduction of bonuses began to change this culture and income disparities widened. There were generally big differences between cities on the coast – in the Special Economic Zones – and inland. Lifestyle distinctions also became increasingly generational as young adults living with parents had more disposable income.

Food, that enduring icon of Chinese culture, was subject to the forces of commercialisation. Among the rapid proliferation of restaurants, McDonalds in Beijing represented a link to Western lifestyles as much as a place to eat. Discos and burger meals became affordable luxuries. The first Kentucky Fried Chicken outlet was opened in Beijing in October 1987, and the first McDonalds in April 1992. It was in such places in particular that the growing importance of women, the youth and children as consumers was clear, a result of changes that combined 'nuclearization of the household, rising awareness of independence and sexual equality among women, the waning of patriarchy and the rediscovery of the value of children' (Yan 2000: 225). At the same time, however, women have lost many of the advances made under Mao, as they were the first to be laid off in times of reduced demand for goods and in other areas too there are signs of the re-emergence of practices associated with lack of economic power. In 1989 and 1990, 65,000 people were arrested for abducting and selling women and children.

With the Chinese people's growing wish for independence and national strength, and the rapid decay of Maoist beliefs, the need for continued stability in the CCP has led to the increased reliance on nationalism as a unifying ideology. Geremie Barme argues that Chinese feelings about foreigners were reflected in a 1993 television mini-series called 'Beijing'ers in New York', which was like 'a reprisal of the Boxers without any belief system' (Barme 1996: 184). For many, an equal dialogue with the outside world is seen as impossible. There still exists a 'deep-felt anxiety over material backwardness, military weakness and political inadequacy' (p. 195).

In June 1990 Jiang Zemin promised political reforms which seemed more aimed at soothing international objectors than achieving real progress. Rules to control students were introduced, and crime had doubled in 1989. The number of executions increased as part of a robust anti-crime campaign. The urban 'job waiting' rate was reported as possibly in excess of four per cent in 1990, and the country was reported to have 300 million agricultural labourers but only needed 180 million. Calls came from the Ministry of Personnel and the Ministry for Labour for a national labour insurance system and an unemployment pensions scheme. Measures were undertaken at the same time to stop the mass exodus of rural workers into towns. 1.3 million people were sent back in 1989 and there were plans for the return of a further 900,000 in 1990. The top priority for the government remained education, the increase of state wages and the relief of rural poverty.

Rights and wrongs

Deng's declared policy of openness to the West has exposed China to international criticism concerning human rights issues. These include press and media freedoms, the suppression of protest, enforced abortions, ignoring calls for democracy, illegal detentions and abuse of the death penalty, the future of Taiwan and the status of Tibet. In June 1989 the suppression of protest by armed troops in Tiananmen Square provoked world-wide condemnation of the Chinese government actions.

The launch of Deng's reforms in the late 1970s ushered in a new era of rebellion by writers and artists. They were angered by contradictory messages about new freedoms, contrasting with heavy clampdowns on opinions deemed to be anti-government. For the government, efforts at control have been hampered by the growth of the very technology the new reforms facilitated, with all their new freedoms and opportunities.

The mood of writers in 1984, with the loss of faith in Mao, was similar to that in 1894 and the loss of faith in Confucius. Now they no longer believed in Communism, many of China's writers began looking outward at other political systems. Liu Binyan and Wang Ruowang, writers persecuted as rightists in 1957, insisted that the depiction of real life in fiction had nothing to do with canons of socialist realism imported from the Soviet Union in the 1950s and still being promoted. A report on an investigation of the journals published privately by Chinese citizens in Beijing in winter 1978 recorded that over 30 unofficial journals and pamphlets were published in Beijing alone, and they were also found in other cities. Most were forced to stop publishing in March 1979 and in February 1981 the government proclaimed unofficial journals illegal, followed by mass arrests in April of that year.

The commercialisation of book publishing brought its own brand of problems. Publishers adopted the goal of becoming more audience-responsive in the early 1980s but, unlike magazines, books cannot easily make money from advertising. Moreover, the most popular books are just the ones most likely to be criticised by the government as violating proscriptions against sex, violence, feudal superstition and bourgeois liberalisation in the media. Some writers chose to opt out of the book market altogether, further restricting the output of high-quality writing.

On 5 January 1985 the Party issued a new 'charter' for writers, promising them new rights to 'democracy and freedom' and echoing once more the Hundred Flowers sentiments. Growing unrest was reflected in literary and pictorial arts, films, poems and cartoons. After the Beijing demonstration of January 1987 a new purge of writers began and the government announced new controls over printed matter including ink, paper and presses. 'Troublemakers' were arrested and imprisoned for counter-revolutionary activities and a new national Lei Feng campaign was launched. This self-sacrificing youth that had been used as a model for young people in the Mao era was once again put forward as embodying all the qualities necessary for building the new, modern China.

Following the Beijing demonstrations of 1978, whose leaders had been arrested for 'rehabilitation', a new kind of protest erupted as 'the curtain rose on a great poster movement' (Chen 1982: 11). The Democracy Wall was a 200-yard brick wall in Xidan, west of Tiananmen Square where posters were pasted which attacked policies and the beliefs of individual government officials. Attracting the attention of both the foreign and Chinese press, protesters complained, among other things, of low living standards, unemployment, youths sent to rural areas and now covertly returning to towns, and corrupt and insensitive local officials.

As the open-door policy was approved by the West, keen to take advantage of potential market opportunities afforded by China, there followed an exchange of delegations, encouragement of tourism, toleration of Westernised clothing and a more relaxed atmosphere in general. The resumption of ties with the US was announced in December 1978 and the following year Deng became the first CCP leader to visit America. Deng tolerated the Democracy movement in its early days, partly because his ousted rival Hua Guofeng was criticised for his lack of reforms and close association with the old order, and partly because they operated as a safety valve for all kinds of grievances.

The loss of state control of important belief-forming media has been caused by administrative fragmentation, property rights reform, and technological advancement in the 1980s and 1990s. The number of newspaper and magazine publishers, television stations and individuals with access to telephones, fax machines and modems in China is increasing rapidly. Loss of control is an unexpected consequence of the reform and opening up necessary for economic development. Advertising was important in the shift to a market economy, but the Party did not anticipate the ideological impact – how advertisements create their own ideology of consumption, and the extent to which they are 'comprehensive manifestations of a consumption concept, a way of life and value-orientation of the countries where such merchandise is produced' (Lynch 1999: 57). A rock music subculture movement produced musicians like Cui Jian, whose first album, called 'New Long March Rock', served as a 'kind of soundtrack for the Tiananmen movement' (Jones 1995: 150). Ai Jing's 'My 1997' was the most popular song to emerge from the rock subculture in 1993 and expresses a longing for a materialist future for which Hong Kong is a metaphor.

Commercialisation has overtaken and weakened the film industry. Film studios, distribution companies and even individual theatres are now responsible for their own profit and many are now financed with money from other Chinese enterprises or foreign capital. The aim is to ensure no commercial flops among the twenty or so films produced by a studio each year. As in the book publishing sphere, there is a tendency to fall back on sex, violence and feudal superstition. Few films shown domestically take on sensitive political issues, and most of those that do are shown only at international film festivals. After fulfilling quotas, film workers can make extra money by working on television series, adverts and music videos. Some, as further described below, have resorted entirely to film-making outside the studio system, in many cases illegally.

The breaking up of the film-distribution monopoly enjoyed by the China Film Corporation contributed to pluralisation and commercialisation, but the centralised Film Import-Export company retained a monopoly over the import and distribution of foreign films, including those originating in Hong Kong.

During the 1980s and early 1990s, foreign imports were restricted to sixty films per year, half of which came from Hong Kong, but in April 1995 the Ministry of Radio, Films and Television agreed to drop restrictions, so as to stimulate the home film industry through competition. Film industry officials think this will lead to a big influx of foreign films, but the Ministry says at least ten of the imported films must be 'good' foreign films, to be defined by the Ministry itself however. As Chinese film-makers enter into more co-productions to improve quality, many will be subject to the infiltration of Western ideas and the government's control of ideological messages will be weakened even further.

In the case of Tiananmen, the foreign press were present and able to report because of the anticipated visit of Soviet premier Gorbachev. In the past, the foreign press has been excluded from reporting events in China and the standard of factual reporting in China itself has been unreliable. Editors had lobbied for years for a press law allowing them to report facts without fear of journalists being arrested, and called for a government obligation to make information available. There had been some signs of a more liberal attitude towards press reporting in 1988 but the imposition of martial law on 20 May 1989 brought press freedom to an end.

In China, media reporting often provokes a strong reaction. The Tiananmen incident of June 1989 was the result of events triggered by the reported death of former Party Leader Hu Yaobang on 15 April. Hu was believed to have been sympathetic to liberal reforms. Students were outraged at the lack of reporting of campus demonstrations and promoted press freedom to one of the protest goals. In 1988 there had seemed to be a limited amount of reporting freedom: Chinese television showed some American imports such as 'Little House on the Prairie' and also screened scenes of protesting students in Korea and Burma. There was increasingly factual reporting under the influence of teaching by foreign journalists.

Because of the unreliability of the official media reporting, alternative ways of acquiring information had always been important. 'Dazibao walls', where people posted information and opinion sheets, played an important role in reporting demonstrations. Other sources of information, such as word of mouth, short-wave radios for listening to 'The Voice of America' and the BBC played a part in spreading news. Later on, even fax machines were used to report demonstrations. However, such methods had their risks. Official Party organs in April 1989 warned of harsh measures that would be taken against those who wished to encourage 'turmoil'.

With regard to the Tiananmen events, several newspapers commented favourably on the student's protest and reported factually. After martial law was declared, the return to press control was gradual but relentless – official Party press organs denied there had been a massacre and said the situation had been highly exaggerated by foreign reporters. At home, journalists and presenters were removed from posts if they reported 'wrongly'. The Chinese government were censured for ignoring calls for democratic representation; the repression of 4 June 1989 has been described as the 'last gasp of Chinese despotism in the face of the inexorable spread of Western liberal capitalism' (Des Forges 1993: 21).

China's response to Western criticisms has been less than appeasing. International pressure was exerted by the United Nations Human Rights Commission after Tiananmen Square and China claimed that the armed response was aimed at protecting themselves from overthrow. The question of how far it was an internal matter became a subject for debate. In the meantime there was an embargo on military sales and the suspension of new loans. During successive visits by world leaders the questions of rights has always been on the visitors' agenda and pursued with varying levels of vigour. Both French and Australian delegations published reports criticising control measures in China and expatriate dissidents continue their criticisms and campaigns from abroad.

There is no doubt that the commercial attractions of China, with its huge population of potential consumers of Western-manufactured goods, plays a vital part in the cementing of international relationships. Whilst memories of past exploitation are still strong, the need to attract investment and the current awareness that the West has much to offer is a sign that trade and cultural relationships will take place on a more equal footing.

Calls for democracy

During the 1980s the Chinese government faced increasing demands for democracy. The outbreak of the 'Patriotic Democratic Movement' in Spring 1989 was brought on by the sudden death of the former Party secretary, Hu Yaobang, who had been displaced two years earlier, in January 1987. Having been perceived as liberal in his attitude towards student demands for greater freedom, his death brought thousands of students onto the streets calling for his name to be cleared and for the government to take action to address students' concerns. Deng, previously seen as a reformer, now took a hard line. Great changes in the preceding ten years had left students behind in the general prosperity growth. The youths that had been sent to the countryside during the Cultural Revolution – 17 million of them since 1967 – had lost their chance of higher education and many illegally returned to the cities where they were unable to find work and so resorted to criminal activity. They had witnessed rural poverty as well as corruption and bullying by local officials. Perceiving themselves to be the successors to the May Fourth movement that began in 1919, they called themselves the April Fifth movement. Whilst they had some knowledge of foreign thinkers, the main influence on their opposition to feudalistic-style authority was their own experience. As early as December 1979 there were demonstrations by youngsters from Yun'an who had come to Beijing to protest, claiming years of mistreatment in plantations. They were promised improvements, at the same time as other groups were clamouring to return to their home cities. In Shanghai some who had been allowed home for the Spring Festival refused to go back and organised campaigns of civil disobedience. Some of them were older workers who had been sent down at end of the Great Leap Forward when there was no work for them in the city.

Student complaints ranged over a number of issues, including their own poor living conditions, the penetration of Japanese economic ventures in China, privilege-abuse by party members and corruption. As suggested by imprisoned dissident Wei Jingshang, they called for the 'Fifth Modernisation', that of democracy, to be added to Deng's Four Modernisations. They also protested Wei's 15-year prison sentence, imposed in 1979, the reduced opportunities for good jobs, and advanced study as well as rising inflation. There had been a significant rise in English-teaching exam registrations for students wishing to go abroad and a general wish for more intellectual freedom amongst the students, who were by now well-informed about freedoms enjoyed by their Western counterparts. Students were largely from privileged backgrounds but conditions for study were poor, resulting in a number of demonstrations in 1984–86. Rising food prices and Spartan living conditions in student dormitories were further exacerbated by the decision to turn the lights off at 11pm in Beijing University. The lack of expenditure on education reform contrasted with the freedoms enjoyed by rich businessmen.

On 15 April 1989 Hu Yaobang had a heart attack and died. By evening wreaths had been placed by students next to trees and walls in Beijing University, imitated by other universities. On the following Monday a few hundred students went to Tiananmen Square, chanting and placing banners at the foot of memorial to the heroes of the people. They stayed to draw up a petition demanding free speech and the clearing of Hu Yaobang's name, publication of details of Party Leaders' incomes, an increase in education funding and a lifting of restrictions on street demonstrations. They decided to stay on after the presentation of the petition, and were joined by others during a night of unrest. On 22 April the funeral ceremony was held, with Zhao Ziyang giving the eulogy. Outside were 100,000 students in the Square, and some decided to stay. Anti-Deng posters began to appear on campuses. On 25 April Li Peng, Deng and Yang Shangkun decided that an anti-government drive was developing and a small group would be set up to deal with it. They also commissioned an explanatory article in the *People's Daily*: it was expected the article would have an intimidating effect, but larger numbers joined the protest.

Mikhail Gorbachev's visit to Beijing lasted from the 15–18 May and, because of the demonstrators, ceremonies had to be changed, including the ceremony of welcome in Tiananmen Square. Instead, Gorbachev was driven through the crowds of demonstrators. Whilst talks between the Soviets and Chinese went on, the world media focus was increasingly on the demonstrators in the Square. Students established a formal association, began to publish a daily newspaper and, on 13 May, began a hunger strike. There were bitter official debates behind the scenes about what to do. Zhao appeared to support the students, with Li against. Yao and Li called for martial law. Zhao, accompanied by Li, addressed students and apologised that he had come too late: he had been absent on an official visit to Korea. Martial law was imposed on 20 May, signed by Li Peng, banning processions, boycotts and strikes, authorising the army to act as it saw fit, and preventing Chinese and foreign press from filming or reporting from the martial law area. On 21 May came a television announcement that the army would not act against students and on 23 May messages were sent to Party headquarters from retired officers saying the PLA could not act against the Chinese people and should not enter the capital. However, the army did enter Beijing during the night of 3–4 June.

Several hundred civilians were killed and thousands wounded as tanks headed to the Square. Tensions ran high because of provocations by the military, including raids to recover 'lost' weapons, and barricades had been built across main roads. Official figures for civilian casualties were not higher than 40, whilst figures for soldiers and policemen exceeded 3,000. It was claimed they acted with restraint. There were official media reports of rioters beating soldiers, who resorted to self-protection by shooting. A television news report showed leaders Deng Xiaoping, Li Peng and Yang Sangkung apparently satisfied about the course of events, and many well-known intellectuals appeared to support the action taken by the authorities. However, although Deng did not comment on television on those who had given orders he was believed to be angry at the bungling manner in which it had occurred and at the indiscriminate firing. When Zhao Ziyang was replaced it was not with Li Peng, who had decreed martial law, but Jiang Zemin, Party Secretary and Mayor of Shanghai.

The media had an influential role to play in the course of events. The editorial of the *People's Daily* on 26 April, commissioned by the government, had inflamed students even more by telling them to return to classrooms. In May, students had the support of people from all walks of life and media coverage of events was extensive. After 4 June there was a blackout of television news for several days, but later in June the names of those wanted for arrest were made public, although many had already left. On 9 June Deng was seen on television addressing commanders, praising troops and policemen who had died as 'heroes'.

Case study: Xiao Wu

A group of directors emerged out of the changing cultural climate of post-Tiananmen China, intent on documenting the society they lived in. The films of what has since become known as the 'Sixth Generation', were a reaction to the social conditions present in modern day China and an artistic rebellion against the style of film favoured by Fifth Generation. Though covered in more depth in the next chapter, the following analysis looks at one Sixth Generation film and how it attempted to highlight issues that have been mentioned in this chapter.

Xiao Wu (1997) tells the story of a pickpocket unwilling to mend his ways. Although warned by a Fenyang's police chief, spurned by his friend, a former pickpocket who has since prospered as a 'legitimate' businessman, and disowned by his father, Xiao Wu refuses to become a part of a society whose values he has no respect for. After being refused entry into his former friend's wedding, with his money gift thrown back at him, Xiao Wu visits a karaoke bar-cum-brothel, where he befriends a hostess, Mei Mei. Entering into a relationship with her, he buys himself a pager so she can keep in contact with him. When he next visits the bar, he discovers that Mei Mei has gone away with clients, leaving no indication of where she has gone or when she will return.

Escaping to his parents, Xiao Wu no sooner arrives than is castigated by his father for his illegal profession, finally being thrown out of their home, disowned and disgraced. Returning to Fenyang, he goes out to work, only to be caught by his first victim, alerted by the ringer of his pager. Censured by the police chief, who told him to give up his way of life, the final scene shows him handcuffed to a telegraph pole in a street, with the local town looking at him with curiosity and disgust.

Xiao Wu's subject matter was considered unappealing and against public taste by the Chinese authorities, who banned it at the script stage. Director Jia Zhang Ke managed to find money via private investors to complete the film, which, on its release was officially condemned. Filmed on location in the director's hometown of Fenyang, the film draws comparison with the work of the Italian Neorealists, in its almost documentary look and use of non-professional actors. An account of the life of one of China's outcasts, the film refuses to condemn Xiao Wu's lifestyle in any way, although is far from objective in its view of the social conditions in and around the town. Instead, it emphasises the injustice present at the heart of contemporary

Chinese society. As critic Richard Corliss points out, such films are about 'ordinary people: sufferers and inflictors of suffering, men of the street and ladies of the evening. There is little facial or verbal inflection, and few dramatic gestures, unless one is smoking.' Most importantly, Corliss states that 'to be noticed is to risk being denounced. Best to blend into the scenery, to seem a grey person in a grey nation. Or to be a twisted bureaucrat. Only then will you flourish' (Corliss 2001: 10). In *Xiao Wu*, the bureaucrats and their associates do flourish. Xiao Wu's former friend, Xiao Jong, is initially presented as a pillar of the community who has been nominated as a model entrepreneur by the local authorities. Later, it is revealed that Xiao Jong is actually a cigarette trafficker who also has an interest in the local prostitute industry. His association with the local police force and bureaucrats emphasises a world as corrupt as Xiao Wu's own profession, now not necessarily condemned not for being against the law, but because his business runs independently of the system and therefore does not contribute toward it.

The film is also critical of the media, which is seen as a tool of state control. The soundtrack is dominated by media reports and official tannoy announcements, declaring the Fenyang Province authority's intention to eradicate street crime. Through their joint presence on the soundtrack, Jia blurs the boundaries between reporting and propaganda. The media are also physically present in the film. One reporter appears regularly throughout the early part of the film. She first appears interviewing Xiao Jong, congratulating him on his prosperous business and forthcoming marriage. Later in the film, after Xiao Wu has been arrested and sits in the police station watching television, the interview and the marriage are screened, emphasising the different routes the two friends' lives have taken. More significantly, it shows that one can remain a criminal and be rewarded for it, provided he works with the system and not against it. The reporter also appears on the street, interviewing a local police officer about the clampdown on street crimes. When she tries to interview one of Xiao Wu's associates, she is met with silence. Again, this scene shows the collusion between the media and the state, as well as emphasising how separated Xiao and his gang are from society.

The most marked difference between *Xiao Wu* and the previous generation of films lies in its limited use of colours. Filmed with a muted palette,
Fenyang is a grey, drab town. The only colours present are in the karaoke
bar, where people choose to escape their everyday lives. Throughout the
film, Jia inserts perfectly framed shots of the town. Unlike the beautifully
composed shots in the films of Zhang Yimou and Chen Kaige, which may
well intimate at oppression or injustice, but which remain ravishing to the
eye, Jia's shots are devoid of any beauty. A parked bike, a street store and
a discarded chair all point to the banality and hopelessness of present day
society and, as a result, the failure of the state to improve the lot of ordinary
people. Such criticisms are voiced in the film's opening scene. As Xiao Wu
is stealing the wallet of a passenger sat next to him on a bus, the camera
cuts to a portrait of Mao Zedong, hanging from the rear-view mirror. While
refusing to offer any direct link between the two shots, the film's opening,
like the rest of the film, implies a link between the state and Xiao Wu's situation. No easy solution is offered. Instead the film appears to ask people
to look around them and ask why society is the way it is; to search for an
answer, rather than pick a scapegoat who is more the result of a problem
than the cause of it.

6   THE SIXTH GENERATION

Changes resulting from Deng's reforms brought poverty, rising crime and a sense of marginalisation to many Chinese cities, which in turn began to be reflected in films, particularly those made in the late 1990s. Most films continued in the celebratory/propaganda mould, such as the big-budget *The Opium War* (1997) by Fourth Generation director Xie Jin, and the new commercialism in film encouraged a mood of conformism. China Film's monopoly on distribution ended and the 16 state-owned studios were told to find their own sources of funding. Now they are heavily reliant on funds from private investors. Censorship is reputed to be even more inscrutable and unpredictable than before.

At the same time there are signs that directors whose works were banned or heavily censored are being reintegrated into the film industry. Tian Zhuangzhuang, whose last feature, *The Blue Kite* (1993), was attacked by censors, is now reinstated in Beijing studios and produces the work of young directors. He had a small part in *The Making of Steel* (1998), directed by Lu Xuechang, dealing with social problems of modern China including sexual promiscuity, drug-addicted commercial artists and women kept as mistresses by overseas businessmen. It has had a limited release in China.

Other Fifth Generation directors have fared less well, both critically and commercially, in China's changing climate. Chen Kaige's films have become increasingly overblown, bearing little similarity or seeming to say little about the modern Chinese condition. Similarly, Zhang Yimou's attitude to the state appears to have softened. Audiences were less than enthusiastic about *Not One Less* (1999), the first film by Zhang to be heartily endorsed by the authorities. Although, according to one critic, the film 'portrays China awakening to the need to be concerned about its own problems instead of how it is seen from the outside' (Wang 1999: 21), and it presents a bleak portrait of a village school, the upbeat ending provoked accusations by the judges at Cannes that the film is propaganda for the Chinese government. Zhang withdrew the film from the festival, and general opinion was that he had 'sacrificed international integrity for the sake of being shown in China' (Wang 1999: 21).

Zhang's latest offering, *The Road Home* (2000), clearly appeals to a commercial audience and has been acquired by Sony Pictures for international release, but manages to incorporate many of the complexities and ambiguities of Zhang's earlier works. An allegorical story of a son who helps his widowed mother to fulfil an ancient funeral rite, the film reflects popular nostalgia for the family virtues that seem to be disappearing in modern China. However, the film is more soft-centred than his previous work, with an ambiguous ending that could be seen as reactionary.

By contrast, the work of the more popular members of the so-called Sixth Generation seems both more urgent and aware of the changes China is undergoing, both domestically and internationally. Wang Xiaoshai's *So Close To Paradise* (aka *The Vietnamese Girl*) (1999) has been a lot more problematic. Many changes were demanded after it was finished in 1995, and even then it was not released. In fact, the unpredictability of censorship now threatens funding overall. Film professionals have gone so far as to accuse the Film Bureau of 'killing' Chinese cinema. Some films of social criticism are made with official approval, such as Li Shaohong's *Family Portrait* (1992), produced by the Beijing Film Studio; a realistic story about an unemployed man in Beijing who cannot face telling his wife he has lost his job when his factory is replaced by a supermarket. *Mr Zhao* (1998), winner of the Grand Prize in Locarno, is a first feature by Lu Yue, former classmate of Zhang Yimou, for whom he shot *To Live* in 1994. About a man caught between two women and two cultures – traditional and 'new' China – it is said to be 'a major step forward' in mainland Chinese film (Elley 1998: 29).

Jiang Wen, director of *In the Heat of the Sun* (1994), is in process of completing a film set during World War Two. His *Postmen in the Mountains* (1999) won the Air Canada Award as most popular film at the Montreal Film Festival. Focusing on the three-day journey of a father and son and their dog to pick up mail, the film depicts a 'tranquil simplicity of key events' (Rist & Totaro 2000: 11). Traditional values are championed, and although the director, who studied painting and worked for ten years as a designer and art director, says he belongs to the Fifth Generation, he is ten years younger than Zhang Yimou, Chen Kaige and Tian Zhuangzhuang. However, another film about family conflict, *Shower* (1998), appears weak in places because in its attempt to be entertaining it 'looks like a Disney rendition of China' (Wang 2000: 27).

A similar 'taming' effect of commercialism may be seen in the latest films of Zhang Yuan, the former leader of the dissident Sixth Generation underground directors whose career is outlined below. His film *Seventeen Years* (1999) marks Zhang's transition from underground to mainstream, but is seen by Chris Berry as a 'mixed blessing' because it is his most conventional and politically safe to date (Berry 1999: 14). Instead of criticising the harshness of the new society and its problems, it could be seen to be praising the leniency of the penal system. Lacking the raw defects of his earlier films, however, it establishes him as one of the most important talents working within the studio system.

The term 'Sixth Generation' is mainly used of film-makers who emerged in the early 1990s. They were mostly born in the 1960s, so the Cultural Revolution was part of their early childhood. Uninterested in the broad sweep of history, the directors concentrate on personal accounts of young people's experience. Financed by foreign money and with very few of the films distributed in China, they are seen as a part of the more general underground movement which includes print media and performance arts.

Independent film in China only started in the late 1980s, when some film-makers started shooting outside the studio system. The films were mainly of a documentary nature, suited to available resources and conditions. Turning their backs on elaborate allegory, they attracted China's private investment in contrast to foreign investment in Fifth Generation films and were thus made on small budgets. Feature films are almost impossible to make in secret, which is why the documentary mode was so important in new films. *Cinéma vérité* techniques were adopted to avoid voice-over narratives and interpretation is left to the viewer as in early Fifth Generation films.

Wu Wenguang is one of the most prominent of the new documentary film-makers. The lack of access to editing facilities is turned to advantage in the loose style of *Bumming in Beijing/The Last Dreamers* (1990), his debut film about a group of disaffected artists in Beijing. *My Time in the Red Guards* (1993) interviews citizens who were involved in the Cultural Revolution, among them director Tian Zhuangzhuang. A number of documentaries appeared to account for, explain and document the Tiananmen events of June 1989, by both foreign and Chinese film-makers. They include *Moving the Mountain* (1994), directed by Michael Apted; *The Gate of Heavenly Peace* (1995), by Carma Hinton and Richard Gordon; and *The Square* (1995) by Zhang Yuan and Duan Jinchan. They present differing accounts of why the movement towards greater political freedom in China remains so difficult.

By the mid-1990s there were signs of a shift to a more socially concerned position: He Ping's *Red Beads* (1993) focuses on a patient in a mental hospital and his fantasies; Guan Hu's *Dirty Men* (1994) addresses a broader range of social issues although still concerned with rock music and the quest for freedom. Another example is He Jianjun's *Postman* (1995), a depressing tale of social isolation set in a dingy Beijing apartment block.

Wang Xiaoshuai, born in Shanghai in 1956, is a director whose films present stylish and powerful portraits of living conditions in contemporary urban China. His first two films were made illegally outside the studio system and depended on private funding and the freely-donated labour of friends. *The Days* (1993), described more fully below, is based on the experiences of a real-life couple of Beijing artists playing themselves, and shows the stresses experienced by the post-socialist artists and intellectuals in the capital. *Frozen* (1997) (released under the pseudonym of Wu Ming) depicts the self-destruction of an artist in the true story of Qi Lei, a young man who expresses contempt for oppressive Chinese society by self-abasing performance art. Shown in the Cannes Film Festival, *So Close to Paradise* (1999) was a film approved by the China Film Board but the mood of the film shows the difficulties he must have had getting it past the censors. Themes of social disenchantment, frustration and compassion are located within a narrative concerning the rehabilitation of the singer, evidently a prostitute, with the inevitable government-approved happy ending. *Beijing Bicycle* (2001), which draws heavily on Vittorio De Sica's *The Bicycle Thief* (1948), is more expansive than Wang's previous work. Again looking at living and working conditions within China's urban centres, he uses the theft of a bicycle to explore the struggles people of all ages encounter in trying to make a living. The winner of the Special Jury Prize at the Berlin Film Festival, it has raised Wang's profile considerably.

Emerging late as one of the most gifted members of the new wave, Jia Zhang Ke's two films have been rapturously received by international critics and festival audiences. As described in the previous chapter, *Xiao Wu* was banned at the script stage, but was made in secret and released to great acclaim. Jia's second film, partly funded by Japanese director Takeshi Kitano, was radically different in style. An episodic account of a decade of radical cultural reform, *Platform* (2000) tells the story of a group of friends whose band progress from agit-prop in 1979 to the less politically minded Mandarin pop, a decade later. Presented through a series of tableaux, Jia eschews the *vérité* style of his first film, in favour of a more formal approach, allowing the action to unfold slowly. In addition to documenting the changes the band go through, the film shows the gradual shift towards Westernisation amongst the younger generation, and the conflict that results.

Arguably the most talented and prolific of China's 'Sixth Generation' directors, Zhang Yuan has survived bans and blacklists to become a 'legitimate' member of the Chinese film-making establishment. Entering the cinematography department of the Beijing Film Academy in 1985, he graduated in 1989 with a BA in Film and went on to become the 'enfant terrible' of the growing underground of film and media personnel active outside the studio system. His debut film, *Mama* (1991), about a mother's relationship with her retarded son, won both jury and public prizes at the Three Continents Film Festival in Nantes. Its fictionalised-documentary format has become its director's style hallmark. The film's three concurrent storylines – black and white footage of the daily life of its protagonist, video interviews, and documentary footage about a school and an institution for the retarded – achieved a dramatic interaction with reality. The casting of a non-professional actor to play the mother and the use of real locations added to the 'intimate' feel of the film.

A characteristic of this and subsequent work by the director was the thoroughness of advance research which contributed greatly to the film's sense of authenticity. The director has continued to show what the authorities believe is an unhealthy interest in social misfits; he believes that portraying the lives of the marginalised most clearly reveals the dynamics of a society.

Zhang's next feature was *Beijing Bastards* (1993) which tracked the lives of aimless urban youths, interspersing scenes of rock music beach-parties with drinking bouts and violent sex. Largely financed by Beijing rock star Cui Jian, it showcased his performance skills. Zhang went on to make three more music videos for the musician before starting his next, disastrous, project, *Chicken Feathers on the Ground* (1993). By now the authorities were watching him closely, and in 1993 he was fired from the television-financed project after pressure had been brought to bear on the producer. His wife, Ning Dai, also a film-maker, recorded events in a video documentary entitled *A Film is Stopped* (1993). In 1994 both their names appeared on a government blacklist which contained six other directors and a collective. Anyone found helping the named film-makers, either by hiring equipment, providing finance or assistance in any way would be liable to prosecution.

Zhang Yuan's response to this public ban was to make his documentary *The Square* (1995) right under the noses of the representatives of authority in Tiananmen Square. This lucid and controversial film about everyday events in the political heart of China used silence about recent events there to eloquent effect. The fascinating subject did much to compensate for its rambling form and frequent repetitiveness.

Pauline Chen, reviewing other documentaries about the Tiananmen events noted the absence of words and music, only 'incidental noise and snippets of conversation', and a 'lack of explicit judgement or explanation'

(Chen 1996: 18). Whether to avoid censorship, or from aesthetic choice, Zhang uses implicitness, indirectness and apparently unconnected scenes and people. Repeated activity, such as that of workers washing a lamp-post and soldiers drilling, suggests the effort of repression. The invasive presence of the military is crystallised in an incident near the end of the film, when cannon shots to welcome the Estonian President are intercut with civilian faces frozen in fear. '*The Square* shows us more clearly than any of the other documentaries what it is to live under the oppressive regime of China' (Chen 1996: 18).

Co-director Duan Jinchuan, interviewed by Chris Berry, explained how 'nerve-wracking' it was to film in Tiananmen Square, but also how the lack of coordination between the various factions responsible for the Square's maintenance and order meant everyone assumed their filming was legitimate (Berry 1998: 88). He claimed the main source of the idea for *The Square* was Wiseman's *Central Park* (1990), a place with some parallel cultural resonance for Americans.

Zhang's next film, *Sons* (1996), about a dysfunctional family, won a prize at the Rotterdam Film Festival and was a popular success. The film depicted a real family, playing themselves – Zhang's own neighbours in a residential quarter of Beijing. It goes completely against the Chinese tradition of reticence concerning family problems in exposing an alcoholic father's descent into madness and characterises his sons as drunken layabouts. As Chris Berry remarks, this is no 'historical allegory', and 'they don't come much grittier' (Berry 1996: 44).

The family's father was brought from a mental institution for the shoot. It won The Tiger Award and the Fipresci International Critics Prize. The structure presents firstly a family history told through photos and narration, followed by a number of scenes depicting drunken arguments, endlessly repeated. The latter are the film's major weakness. Shot mostly indoors or at night, the project lent itself very well to the need for secrecy.

The title of the director's next film, *East Palace, West Palace* (1997), refers to the public toilets at the side of Tiananmen Square, a cruising spot for gay men in Beijing. There are no laws against homosexuality in China, but gays are liable to censure from forces of local control. Thanks to foreign investment, the film was shot with state-of-the-art lighting equipment, but again was not seen in China. What began as a film about gay lifestyles turned into a psychological drama between authority and victim, with the arresting officer tricked into complicity with the arrested youth. Although the film was completely fictional, Zhang filmed using actual locations. Frustrated when it was banned in Beijing, he toured Europe with a staged adaptation.

In 1999, Zhang's rehabilitaton into the film establishment occurred when the progressive and respected head of Xi'an Film Studio employed him to make *Crazy English* (1999), a documentary about a failed student who became a millionaire after devising an eccentric approach to teaching English to Chinese people. Travelling across China with his stadium road show, Li Yang goads his crowd to shout out basic English and overcome their inhibitions with a preacher's zeal. In the guise of a somewhat repetitive tour of China's top tourist spots and universities Zhang reveals an all-too-exploitable nationalism. In his customary fashion the director lets the subjects speak for themselves.

When, as *Variety* critic Derek Elley notes, Zhang was invited in 'out of the Indie bad-boy cold' (Elley 1999b: 47), it was with a vengeance. His *Seventeen Years* (1999) marginally recalls his debut film *Mama* because of its muted, naturalistic style, and places Zhang in the top ranks of Chinese directors. The film remains a feature whilst drawing on the director's strong documentary interests. The ironic Chinese title *New Year Homecoming* refers to the release of a female prisoner to visit her family after a 17-year sentence for the accidental killing of a favoured sibling in a domestic incident. The accompanying female guard and the prisoner bond during the search for the missing family. The film has convincing dialogue and an excellent musical score by Zhao Jiping. It was the first film to get permission to film inside a Chinese prison – the criminals playing themselves.

The Best Director prize in Venice was seen as a reward for Zhang Yuan's 'tenacity and talent'. Influenced, as they have been in the past, by this international acclaim, the Chinese censors at last gave permission to the director to show one of his films on the mainland, the first of the director's five films to be shown in China, as reported by the *Beijing Morning Post*.

FIGURE 9 *The Days*

It began showing in Beijing at the beginning of December 1999. His other films were not allowed a public showing, it was explained, because they emphasised the dark side of Chinese society.

Case study: The Days

The Days, illegally produced and directed, was made on a shoestring budget of £7,000, donated by private investors, and completed in January 1993 and won the Grand Prix at the 1994 Thessalonika Film Festival. The film presents a depressing portrait of the lives of China's young intellectuals. Alternating between an ugly and comfortless urban apartment block and the bleak landscape of north-western China, the film depicts the final months of the declining relationship of two young artists. Dong and Chun are as incompatible as their names (Winter and Spring) suggest and in charting the stages of the breakdown in their relationship the film shows it is not only their contrasting approaches to their problems which lead to a lack of

FIGURE 10 *The Days*

communication, but the nature of the problems themselves. The style of documentary realism, with grainy black and white photography and voice-over narration, gives a sense of authenticity to the settings and events depicted. The stars of the film are a real-life couple who are also stars of the Beijing art-world – typical artist-intellectuals of the 1990s – feeling alienated from the system on which they depend and struggling to supple-ment a meagre salary. The dismal settings, whether the untidy apartment which doubles as a studio or the stubbled landscape encountered on the disenchanting journey to Dong's parental home, add to the general sense of desolation. A series of metaphors underscores the mood, such as the burnt-off fields in the rural landscape which parallel empty existences, and the squads of students in military training who jog past the block each morning and emphasise the depressing routine and the rigidity of society.

The explicit love-making in the opening scene, enough in itself to cause the film to be banned, is mechanical and unerotic. Compared with the more wide-reaching social concerns of Fifth Generation directors, Wang's film is an intimate account of day-to-day life as lived by himself and contempo-raries, a moving account of the end of a relationship which also pinpoints a general mood of dread and incipient defeat.

Through their words and actions, the protagonists depict the ills of their society. Chun's irritation as she tries to cook and do laundry with broken-down equipment is readily transformed into resentment of her partner. The mental stress endured by Dong is apparent in his chain-smoking and alcohol dependence. Unable to respond to his wife's appeal for emotional reassurance, he notes the passage of time marked by his greying hair. Dong dreams of selling his paintings to rich foreigners, but fails. His painting spells are interspersed with press-ups, echoing the military motif estab-lished by the young soldiers who jog past the apartment block. His response to his wife's news that she is pregnant is to say she can give birth in the US and get a residence permit, but instead she has an abortion in a clinic. That their situation is not unique is underlined by the queues at the clinic, a reflection of the government's quota policy on childbirth. Dong's feeling of alienation are paralleled by the experience of a college friend who joins him on a drinking binge. His companion, who apparently tried to leave the country but failed, tells him his work-unit continued to pay his salary for a year since nobody noticed he had gone.

Dung and Chun are separated from parents who have been disgraced for class reasons during the Cultural Revolution. Nostalgia for a lost past is a recurring theme but the past has been destroyed, as is demonstrated in the visit to Dong's childhood home. Although initially elated by the journey, the disorientation they feel on arrival signals a further disillusion. Dong's old school is deserted and the playground abandoned. In Dong's parents' apartment his incipient traditional sexism is strengthened, and Chun finally leaves.

The breakdown of traditional family roles and status is reflected in the portrayal of the parents. Although cushioned by a pension, the father has lost the traditional patriarchal status and has little to occupy him, whilst the mother is relegated to endlessly cleaning an already spotless tiny flat. Back in Beijing, Dong finds little comfort in a letter from Chun in the US that tells him, 'This is what life should really be like'. In a final significant irony, the psychiatrist tells Dong, after he has a minor breakdown and smashes glass in the university building, that his case is not so uncommon.

CONCLUSION

At the present time the way ahead for a cinema which is distinctly Chinese is uncertain. In his introduction to a series of essays which questions the notion of a national cinema, Sheldon Lu states: 'China's film industry is caught in the throes of a transition from a state-controlled system to a market mechanism. National cinema suffers from a decline in funding and the audience and is in deep crisis' (Lu 1997: 9). The old state-funding system which produced the quality of films of the Fifth Generation ensured guaranteed work for employees, whilst box-office success and film marketing were irrelevant: it was the government's role to decide which films would be made and ensure distribution to a populace it was determined to 'educate' through the film medium.

The Chinese government is still willing to fund projects that it approves. However, there has been a decline in actual film-making by studios, who have been forced to look to other means of raising revenue. These methods include selling their 'banners' to independently made films, making soaps for an expanding content-hungry television industry, and co-producing and co-financing with foreign or domestic independent companies. Joint productions can be problematic and are at least as commercially driven in terms of pleasing an international audience as films which cater for the tastes of the mainland Chinese and other Asian audiences.

The studios also face the twin threat of an increasing quota of expensively made American films capturing the domestic audience, especially after China's imminent entry into the World Trade Organisation and further expansion of quotas for foreign films.

If, as Lu claims, 'Internationalism as such is a way both to evade and to defy the internal domination of the regime' (Lu 1997: 11), it also provided in the past for the protection of directors who sailed close to the wind in terms of offending the government. On the other hand, the international success of the films of the Fifth Generation at Film Festivals attracted the attention of the global audience and fuelled a demand for films of a similar high quality. As has been argued, it was partly their experiences of dramatic social change and partly the restrictions placed upon them by censorship, together with some exposure to European films, that caused them to seek a new film language in which to express their concerns about Chinese society.

Shaoyi Sun (2000) points out three main groups of directors now operating legally in China, each group having distinct aims and sources of revenue. Of the first group are Zhang Yimou and Chen Kaige, who have no problems attracting foreign investment. Zhang's *The Road Home* (2000), for instance, was heavily funded by the Sony Corporation and was very favorably received both in China and abroad, whilst Kaige's *The Emperor and the Concubine* was the most expensive film made in Asia, again heavily reliant on Japanese money. Another group of directors are happy to make government-approved films which promote official interpretations of historical events, of which veteran director Xie Jin's *The Opium War* (1997) and Wu Ziniu's eloquently named *National Anthem* (1999) are recent examples. The third group are film-makers who are willing to consider the tastes of domestic audiences and aim for box-office success. They include Feng Xiaogang, whose film *Part A, Part B* (1997), starring Ge You, 'best actor' star of Zhang Yimou's *To Live*, set a box-office record in China.

The Sixth Generation independents, suggests Sun, despite help from some Fifth Generation film-makers, are too often driven to give up their 'big-screen dream' (Sun 2000: 4) and resort to television work. However, this experience has led at least one of them to make the innovative and intriguing glimpse of Shanghai life offered in *Suzhou River* (2000), a winner at the Rotterdam International Film Festival.

This book has been concerned with mainland films, and it was the Fifth Generation films which created a demand for films reflecting Chinese mainland experience, particularly where the themes were set in the exotic past and involved forced marriage or oppressive social conditions. Ironically, this demand has been met by a growth in opportunities for Hong Kong and Taiwanese directors such as Ang Lee and Wong Kar-wai, or American-dwelling John Woo, Wayne Wang and, more recently, Chen Kaige. Clara Law, the Australian-based Chinese director, is another whose films about the Chinese diaspora have an international audience, albeit smaller than the aforementioned.

The emergence of China as a twenty-first-century world power and trading nation will also be reflected in the increased interest in films and film-making. There has already been a rapid rise of Chinese cinema studies in Western academia. China's colonial past, argues Lu, means Chinese cinema was essentially transnational from the first. However, Edward Yang's latest film, *A One and a Two* (2000), superb in many respects, demonstrates all too clearly what can be lost – Taipei and Tokyo are repackaged for tourists, and the cameo Japanese businessman all but wears a halo. Ang Lee's *Crouching Tiger, Hidden Dragon* (2000), for all its authentic Chinese landscape and Qing Dynasty setting, owes more to the Hong Kong kung fu genre than to the Chinese mainland film tradition. On the other hand, Zhang Yimou's *The Road Home* (2000) can be best understood against a background of Confucian values, a troubled political past and a nostalgia for disappearing processes and customs. It remains to be seen whether this film will be the swan song of a recognisable Chinese cinema.

FILMOGRAPHY

Army Nurse (*Nuer Lou*) (Hu Mei, 1985, Ch.)

The Artist Qi Baishi (*Qi Baishi Huajia*) (1955, Ch.)

Beijing Bastards (*Beijing Zazhong*) (Zhang Yuan, 1993, Ch.)

Beijing Bicycle (*Shiqi Sui De Dan Che*) (Xiaoshuai Wang, 2001, Fr./Ch.)

Beijing'ers in New York (*Beijingren zai niuyue*) (television serial) (Zheng Xiaolong, 1993, Ch.)

Bells Ring in Green Valley (*Cui gu Zhongsheng*) (Liu Qiong, 1958, Ch.)

The Bicycle Thief (Vittoria De Sica, 1948, It.)

The Big Parade (King Vidor, 1925, US)

The Big Parade (*Da Yueb Bing*) (Chen Kaige, 1985, Ch.)

The Bitter Tea of General Yen (Frank Capra, 1932, US)

Bloody Morning (*Xuese Qingchen*) (Li Shaohong, 1990, Ch.)

The Blue Kite (*Lan Fengzheng*) (Tian Zhuangzhuang, 1993, HK)

Breaking the Silence (*Piaoliang Mama*) (Sun Zhou, 2000, Ch.)

Breaking with Old ideas (*Juelie*) (Li Wenhua, 1975, Ch.)

The Bridge (*Qiao*) (Wang Pin, 1949, Ch.)

Broken Arrow (John Woo, 1996, US)

Broken Blossoms (D. W. Griffiths, 1919, US)

Broken Fetters (B. Lopoknysh, 1916, USSR)

Bumming in Beijing/ The Last Dreamers (*Liulang Beijing/Zuihou de Mengxiangzhe*) (Wu Wegang, 1990, Ch.)

Burma Convoy (Noel Mason Smith, 1941, US)

Capture Mount Hua by Stratagem (*Zhiqu Huashan*) (Guo Wei, 1953, Ch.)

Cat on a Hot Tin Roof (Richard Brooks and James Poe, 1958, US)

Central Park (Frederick Wiseman, 1990, US)

Cheng the Fruit Seller (aka *Labourer's Love*) (*Zhiguo Yuan/Laogong Zhi Aiqing*) (Zhang Shichuan, 1922, Ch.)

Chicken Feathers on the Ground (Yi Di Ji Mao) (Zhang Yuan, 1993, Ch.)

Chin Miao (*Chunmiao*) (Xie Jin, 1975, Ch.)

China Fights Back (Harry Dunham, 1941, US)

China Girl (Abel Ferrera, 1987, US)

China Seas (Tony Garnett, 1935, US)

Chinese Box (Wayne Wang, 1997, Fr./Jap.)

Chungking Express (*Chongqing Senlin*) (Wong Kar-Wai, 1994, HK)

City without Night (*Buye Cheng*) (Tang Xiaodan, 1957, Ch.)

Cocaine (Graham Cutts, 1922, UK)

Codename Cougar (*Daihao Meizhou Bao*) (Zhang Yimou, 1989, Ch.)

The Corner Forsaken by Love (*Bei Aiqing Yiwang Di Jialuo*) (Zhang Qi and Li Yalin, 1981, Ch.)

Crazy English (*Fenkuang Yingyu*) (Zhang Yuan, 1999, Ch.)

Crouching Tiger, Hidden Dragon (*Wo Hu Zang Long*) (Ang Lee, 2000, TW/US)

Crows and Sparrows (*Wuya Yu Maque*) (Zheng Junli, 1949, Ch.)

Daughters of China (*Zhonghua Nuer*) (Ling Zifeng and Zhai Qiong, 1949, Ch.)

Daughter of the Party (*Dangde Nuer*) (Lin Nong, 1958, Ch.)

The Days (*Dongchun de Rizi*) (Wang Xiaoshuai, 1993, Ch.)

The Descendants of Confucius (*Jueli Renjia*) (Wu Yigong, 1992, Ch.)

The Difficult Couple (*Nanfu Nanqi*) (Zhang Shichuan and Zheng Zhengqiu, 1913, Ch.)

Dirt (*Toufa Luanle*) (Guan Hu, 1994, Ch.)

Dislocation (aka *The Stand-in*) (*Guo Wei*) (Huang Jianxin, 1986, Ch.)

Doctor Bethune (*Bai Qiuen daifu*) (Zhang Junxian, 1964, Ch.)

Dong Cunrui (*Dong Cunrui*) (Guo Wei, 1955, Ch.)

Dragon Seed (Harold S. Bucquet, 1944, US)

Dragon's Beard Ditch (*Long Xu Gou*) (Xian Qun, 1952, Ch.)

Drive to Win (*Sha Ou*) (Zhang Nuanxin, 1981, Ch.)

Drum Singers (aka *Travelling Players*) (*Gushu Yiren*) (Tian Zhuangzhuang, 1987, Ch.)

The Dying Rooms (Kate Blewett, 1995, UK)

Early Spring in February (*Zaochun Eryue*) (Xie Tieli, 1963, Ch.)

East Palace, West Palace (*Donggong, Xigong*) (Zhang Yuan, 1997, Ch.)

The Emperor and the Assassin (*Jing Ke Ci Qin Wang*) (Chen Kaige, 1999, Ch.)

The Emperor's Shadow (*Qin Song*) (Zhou Xiaowen, 1996, Ch./HK)

Ermo (*Er Mo*) (Zhou Xiawwen, 1994, Ch./HK)

Family Portrait (*Si shi bu huo*) (Li Shaohong, 1992, Ch./HK)

Farewell My Concubine (*Ba Wang Bie Ji*) (Chen Kaige, 1993, HK)

A Film is Stopped (*Yi Bu Yingpian Wei Wancheng Yinqi De Taolun*) (Ning Dai, 1993, Ch.)

The First Sino-Japanese War (*Jia Wu Feng Yun*) (Wang Jiayi, 1962, Ch.)

Five Golden Flowers (*Wu Duo Jin Hua*) (Wang Jiayi, 1959, Ch.)

Forrest Gump (Robert Zemeckis, 1994, US)

Frozen (*Jidu Hanleng*) (Wu Ming, 1997, HK/NL/Ch.)

The Gate of Heavenly Peace (Carma Hinton and Richard Gordon, 1995, US)

The General Died at Dawn (Lewis Milestone, 1936, US)

A Girl from Hunan (*Xiannu Xiao Xiao*) (Xie Fei, 1986, Ch.)

The Girls from Shanghai (*Shanghai guniang*) (Cheng Yi, 1958, Ch.)

The Great Conqueror's Concubine (*Xi Chu Bawang*) (Stephen Shin, 1994, HK)

The Good Earth (Sidney A. Franklin, 1936, US)

Happy Together (*Chunguang Zhaxie*) (Wong Kar-Wai, 1997, HK)

Hell and High Water (Stephen Bekassy, 1954, US)

Heroic Sons and Daughters (*Yingxiong Ernu*) (Wu Zhaodi, 1964, Ch.)

Hibiscus Town (*Furong Zhen*) (Xie Jin, 1986, Ch.)

High School Confidential (Jack Arnold, 1958, US)

Horse Thief (*Daoma Zei*) (Tian Zhuangzhuang, 1985, Ch.)

In the Heat of the Sun (*Yangguang Canlan de Rizi*) (Jiang Wen, 1994, Ch.)

Ju Dou (Zhang Yimou, 1990, Ch./Jap.)

Keep Cool (*You Hua Hao Hao Shuo*) (Zhang Yimou, 1997, HK/TW)

The Keys of the Kingdom (John M. Stahl, 1944, US)

The Killer (*Diexue Shuang Xiong*) (John Woo, 1989, HK)

Killing Me Softly (Chen Kaige, 2001, UK)

King of the Children (*Haizi Wang*) (Chen Kaige, 1987, Ch.)

Kundun (Martin Scorsese, 1997, US)

Lenin in 1918 (*Lenin V 1918 Godo*) (Mikhail Romm, 1939, USSR)

Lenin in October (*Lenin V Voktyabre*) (Mikhail Romm, 1937, USSR)

Li Lianying: The Imperial Eunuch (*Da Tai Jian Li Lian Ying*) (Tian Zhuangzhuang, 1991, Ch./HK)

Li Shuangshuang (*Li Shuangshuang*) (Lu Ren, 1962, Ch.)

The Life of Wu Xun (*Wu Xun Chuan*) (Sun Yu, 1950, Ch.)

Life on a String (*Bian Zou Bian Chang*) (Chen Kaige, 1991, Ch./Ger./Jap.)

Limehouse Blues (Alexander Hall, 1934, US)

The Lin Family Shop (*Lin Jia Puzhi*) (Shui Hua, 1959, Ch.)

The Lion King (Roger Allers, 1994, US)

Little House on the Prairie (television series) (Leo Penn, 1974–5, US)

Little Toys (*Xiao Wanyi*) (Sun Yu, 1933, Ch.)

Long Love the Mistress (*Taitai Wansui*) (Sang Hu, 1947, Ch.)

The Making of Steel (*Zhangda Chengren*) (Lu Xuechang, 1998, Ch.)

Mama (Zhang Yuan, 1991, Ch.)

Mary from Beijing (*Mengxing Shifan*) (Zhang Aijia and Sylvia Chang, 1993, Ch./HK)

The Mating Game (George Marshall, 1958, US)

Mr Wu (Maurice Elvey, 1920, UK)

Mr Zhao (*Zhao Xiansheng*) (Lu Yue, 1998, Ch./HK)

Moving the Mountain (Michael Apted, 1994, US)

My Time in the Red Guards (*Wo de Hongweining Shidai*) (Wu Wenguang, 1993, Ch.)

National Anthem (Wu Ziniu, 1999, Ch.)

New Heroes and Heroines (*Xin Er Nu Ying Xiong Zhuan*) (Lu Ban, 1951, Ch.)

Not One Less (*Yige Dou Buneng Shao*) (Zhang Yimou, 1999, Ch.)

Oil for the Lamps of China (Mervyn LeRoy, 1935, US)

Old Well (*Lao Jing*) (Tian-Ming Wu, 1986, Ch.)

On the Hunting Ground (*Liechang Zasa*) (Tian Zhuangzhuang, 1985, Ch.)

One and Eight (*Yige he Bage*) (Zhang Junzhao, 1984, Ch.)

A One and a Two (*Yi Yi*) (Edward Yang, 2000, TW/Jap.)

The Opium War (*Lin Zexu*) (Zheng Junli, 1959, Ch.)

The Opium War (*Yapian Zhanzheng*) (Xie Jin, 1997, Ch.)

Our Niu Baisui (, 1984, Ch.)

Part A, Part B (Feng Xiaogang, 1997, Ch.)

Platform (*Zhantai*) (He Yi, aka Jia Zhang Ke, 2000, HK/Jap./Fr.)

Postmen in the Mountains (*Nashan, Naren, Nagou*) (Jiang Wen, 1999, Ch.)

Raise the Red Lantern (*Da Hong Donlong Gaogaogua*) (Zhang Yimou, 1991, Ch.)

Rebecca (Alfred Hitchcock, 1940, US)

Red Beads (*Xuan Lian*) (He Ping, 1993, Ch.)

The Red Detachment of Women (*Hongse Niangzijun*) (Xie Jin, 1961, Ch.)

Red Firecracker, Green Firecracker (*Pao Da, Shuang Deng*) (He Ping, 1993, HK/Ch.)

Red Sorghum (*Hong Gaoliang*) (Zhang Yimou, 1988, Ch.)

Regret for the Past (*Shangshi*) (Shui Hua, 1981, Ch.)

Rendezvous at Orchid Bridge (*Lanqiao Wei*) (Xie Jin, 1954, Ch.)

Reverberations of Life (*Shenghuo de Chanyin*) (Teng Wenji and Wu Tianming, 1979, Ch.)

Revolutionary Family (*Geming jiating*) (Shui Hua, 1961, Ch.)

Rickshaw Boy (*Luotuo Xiangzi*) (Ling Zifeng, 1982, Ch.)

River Elegy (*Heshang*) (television series) (Su Xiaokang and Wang Luxiang, 1988, Ch.)

The Road Home (*Wode Fu qin, Muqin*) (Zhang Yimou, 2000, Ch.)

Rock n'Roll Kids (*Yaogun Qingnian*) (Tian Zhuangzhuang, 1988, Ch.)

Rouge (*Yanzhi Kou*) (Stanley Kwan, 1987, HK)

Savage Land (*Yuan Ye*) (Ling Zi, 1981, Ch.)

Secret Decree (*Die Xue Hei Gu*) (Wu Ziniu, 1985, Ch.)

Serfs (*Nongnu*) (Li Jun, 1964, Ch.)

Seventeen Years (*Guonian Huijia*) (Zhang Yuan, 1999, Ch.)

Shanghai Bound (Luther Reed, 1927, US)

The Shanghai Gesture (Josef von Sternberg, 1942, US)

Shanghai Triad (*Yao a Yao Yao dao Waipoqiao*) (Zhang Yimou, 1995, Ch.)

Shower (*Xizao*) (Zhang Yang, 1998, Ch.)

Sisters Stand Up (*Jie Jie Mei Mei Zhan Qi lai*) (Chen Xihe, 1951, Ch.)

So Close To Paradise (aka *The Vietnamese Girl*) (*Biandan Guniang*) (Wang Xiashuai, 1999, Ch.)

Song of the Fishermen (*Yuguangqu*) (Cai Chusheng, 1935, Ch.)

Song of Youth (*Qingchun zhi Ge*) (Cui Wei and Chen Huaiai, 1959, Ch.)

Soul of a Painter (*Hua Hun*) (Huang Shuqin, 1993, Ch./TW)

Sons (*Erzi*) (Zhang Yuan, 1996, Ch.)

Suzhou River (*Suzhou He*) (Ye Lou, 2000. Ch./Ger.)

Spring in a Small Town (*Xiaocheng Zhi Chun*) (Fei Mu, 1948, Ch.)

A Spring River Flows East (*Yi Jiang Chunsu Xiang Dong Liu*) (Cai Chusheng and Zheng Junli, 1947, Ch.)

Spring Silkworm (Cheng Bugou, 1933, Ch.)

The Square (*Guangchang*) (Zhang Yuan and Duan Jinchan, 1995, Ch.)

Stage Sisters (aka *Two Stage Sisters*) (*Wutai Jiemei*) (Xie Jin, 1965, Ch.)

The Story of Qiu Ju (*Qiu Ju Da Guanxi*) (Zhang Yimou, 1992, HK/Ch.)

Tell it to the Marines (George W. Hill, 1927, US)

Temptress Moon (*Feng Yue*) (Chen Kaige, 1996, HK)

Terracotta Warrior (*Qin Yong*) (Cheng Xiaodong, 1990, Can./HK)

Third Sister Liu (*Lu San Jie*) (Su Li, 1960, Ch.)

A Thousand Miles a Day (*Yi Ri Qian Li*) (Yan Jizhou, 1958, Ch.)

The Tunnel of Love (Gene Kelly, 1958, US)

Tunnel Warfare (*Di daozhan*) (Chen Yin, 1952, Ch.)

To Live (*Huozhe*) (Zhang Yimou, 1994, HK/Ch.)

Twin Sisters (*Zimei Hua*) (Zheng Zhengqiu, 1933, Ch.)

Woman Basketball Player No 5 (*Nu Lan Wu Hao*) (Xie Jin, 1957, Ch.)

Xiao Wu (Jia Zhang Ke, 1997, HK/Ch.)

Yang + Yin: Gender in Chinese Cinema (Stanley Kwan, 1996, HK/UK)

A Yank on the Burma Road (George B. Seitz, 1942, US)

Year of the Dragon (Michael Cimino, 1985, US)

The Yellow Claw (Rene Plaisetty, 1920, UK)

Yellow Earth (*Huang Tudi*) (Chen Kaige, 1984, Ch.)

The Yellow Menace (William Steiner, 1916, US)

Yesterday's Wine (*Yu Wangshi Ganbei*) (Xia Gang, 1995, Ch.)

Young Masters of the Great Leap Forward (*Da Yue Jin Zhong De Xiao Zhu Ren*)
　　(Xie Jin, 1958, Ch.)

BIBLIOGRAPHY

The bibliography lists works cited in the text and is also designed to point to useful further reading. The annotated list of 'essential reading' highlights works considered to be of particular importance to the field of New Chinese Cinema while the 'secondary reading' list includes many other works of interest for further research.

ESSENTIAL READING

Berry, Chris (ed.) (1991) *Perspectives on Chinese Cinema*. London: BFI.
> *This excellent collection of essays offers close readings of some key films of the Fifth Generation directors. It also includes historical and cultural perspectives on early Chinese cinema and biographical accounts of leading directors.*

Chow, Rey (1995) *Primitive Passions: Visuality, Sexuality, Ethnography and Contemporary Chinese Cinema*. New York: Columbia University Press.
> *A multi-disciplinary approach to Chinese films of the Sixth Generation directors which strongly repays the effort to read the author's densely-written prose. It offers valuable insights into the relationship between film and Chinese culture as well as examining how film relates to other media.*

Clark, Paul (1989) *Chinese Cinema: Culture and Politics since 1949*. Cambridge: Cambridge University Press.
> *This detailed account of the growth of the Chinese film industry shows how the influence of film-makers, politics and audience combine to make a distinctive Chinese cinema.*

Ebrey, Patricia B. (1999) *The Cambridge Illustrated History of China*. Cambridge: Cambridge University Press.
> *A very readable, lavishly illustrated overview of Chinese history and culture delivered in accessible sections which make it an excellent reference book.*

Leyda, Jay (1972) *Dianying: An Account of Films and the Film Audience in China*. Cambridge, MA: MIT Press.

A full account of the growth of the film industry from its early days which gives a fascinating sense of social setting of the cinema in China.

Lu, Sheldon H. (ed.) (1997) *Transnational Chinese Cinemas: Identity, Nation, Gender*. Honolulu: University of Hawaii Press.
A collection of essays which engages with the internationalisation of Chinese films of the mainland and the wider Chinese diaspora. It engages with a number of contemporary debates in tracing the relationship of national cinema to global capitalism.

Marion, Donald J. (1997) *The Chinese Filmography 1949–1995*. Jefferson: MacFarland.
This useful reference work contains synopses and production details of Chinese mainland films since 1949 with a short historical overview at the beginning.

Tam, Kwok-Kan and Wimal Dissanayake (1998) *New Chinese Cinema*. Hong Kong: Oxford University Press.
This lucid collection of studies of the work of contemporary film-makers is based on interviews with leading New Wave directors from the mainland, Taiwan and Hong Kong. It also features some very good stills and location shots, many in colour.

Zhang, Yingjin and Zhiwei Xiao (1998) *An Encyclopaedia of Chinese Film*. London: Routledge.
This invaluable reference book includes plot synopses, production details and comments for all studio-made Chinese films, including those for Hong Kong and Taiwan. It also includes information on independent directors.

SECONDARY READING

AFP (1999) 'Yuan Wins Approval to Show Films in China', *Asian Age*, 14 Dec, 18.

Amnesty International (1991) *China, Punishment Without Crime, Administrative Detention*. London: Amnesty International.

Andors, Phyllis (1983) *The Unfinished Liberation of Chinese Women*. Bloomington: Indiana University Press.

Barme, Geremie R. (1996) 'To Screw Foreigners is Patriotic: China's Avant-garde Nationalists', in Jonathan Unger (ed.) *Chinese Nationalism*. New York: M.E. Sharp, 183–208.

Benewick, Robert and Paul Wingrove (1995) *China in the 1990s*. London: Macmillan.

Benson, Michael (1997) 'Market Stalinism', *Sight and Sound*, June, 5.

Berlin, Michael J. (1993) 'The Performance of the Chinese Media During the Beijing Spring' in Roger V. Des Forges, Luo Ning and Wu Yen-Bo (eds) *Chinese Democracy and the Crisis of 1989: Chinese and American Reflections*. New York: State University of New York Press, 263–75.

Berry, Chris (1989) 'Now You See It, Now You Don't', *Cinemaya*, Summer, 47–55.

____ (1993) 'At What Price Success', *Cinemaya*, Summer, 20–3.

____ (1994) 'A Nation T(w/o)o: Chinese cinema(s) and Nationhood(s)' in Wimal Dissanayake (ed.) *Colonialiam and Nationalism in Asian Cinema*. Bloomington: Indiana University Press, 42–64.

____ (1995) 'Hidden Truths', *Cinemaya*, 28–9, 52.

____ (1996) Review of *Erzi*, *Cinemaya*, Spring, 44.

____ (1996) 'Box Office Revolution: Hong Kong and the Transformation of the Chinese Film Industry', *Cinema Papers*, 111, 27.

_____ (1997) 'Crossing the Wall', *Dox: Documentary Film Quarterly*, 13, 14–15.

_____ (1998) 'We live in a country of earthquakes': China's Independent Documentary Filmmakers', *Metro*, 113/14, 86–7.

_____ (1998) Interview with Duan Jinchuan, *Metro*, 113/14, 88–9.

_____ (1999) Interview with Duan Jinchuan, *Cinemaya* 28–9, 140–6.

Bin, Zhao (1994) '*The China Syndrome*', *Sight and Sound*, August, 34.

Browne, Nick, Paul G. Pickowicz, Vivian Sobchack and Esther Yau (eds) (1994) *New Chinese Cinemas: Forms, Identities, Politics*. Cambridge: Cambridge University Press.

Byars, Jackie (1991) *All That Hollywood Allows: Reading Gender in 1950s Melodrama*. London: Routledge.

Callahan, William A. (1993) 'Gender, Ideology, Nation: *Ju Dou* in the Cultural Politics of China', *East-West Film Journal*, 7, 1, 52–80.

Chang, Jung (1991) *Wild Swans: Three Daughters of China*. London: HarperCollins.

Chen, Pauline (1996) 'Screening History: New Documentaries on the Tiananmen Events in China', *Cineaste*, 22, 4, 18.

Chen, Ruoxi (1982) *Democracy Wall and the Unofficial Journals*. Berkeley: University of California.

Cheng, Scarlet (1996) '*The China Syndrome*', *Scanorama*, March, 37–40.

_____ (1997) 'China's Garbo?', *Interview*, May, 54–6.

Cheshire, Godfrey (1994) 'Chinese Checkers', *Film Comment*, 3, 4, 65.

Chi, Pen (ed.) (1977) *Chinese Women in the Fight for Socialism*. Peking: Foreign Languages Press.

Chow, Rey (1991) *Woman and Chinese Modernity: The Politics of Reading Between East and West*. Minneapolis: University of Minnesota Press.

Clegg, Jenny (1994) *Fu Manchu and the 'Yellow Peril': The Making of a Racist Myth*. Stoke-on-Trent: Trentham Books.

Corliss, Richard (2001) *Time International*, 26 March, 10.

Cotterell, Arthur (1993) *East Asia: From Chinese Predominance to the Rise of the Pacific Rim*. London: John Murray.

Crantur, Jean-Marc and Florence Le Borgne (1999) *The World Film and Television Market*. Montpellier: Institut de l'Audiovisuel et des Telecommunications en Europe.

Croll, Elisabeth (1995) *Changing Identities of Chinese Women: Rhetoric, Experience and Self-Perception in Twentieth-Century China*. Hong Kong: Hong Kong University Press.

Dalrymple, James (1995) 'Republic Enemy No 1', *Sunday Times Colour Supplement*, 6 August, 16–21.

Davenport, Hugo (1994) 'Epic Drama on History's Stage', *Daily Telegraph*, 7 January, 6.

David, Mohan D. (1993) *The Making of Modern China*. Bombay: Himalaya Publishing House.

Davis, Deborah S. (2000) *The Consumer Revolution in Urban China*. Berkeley: University of California Press.

Des Forges, Roger V. (1993) 'Democracy in Chinese History', in Roger V. Des Forges, Luo Ning & Wu Yen-bo (eds) *Chinese Democracy and the Crisis of 1989: Chinese and American Reflections*. Albany, NY: State University of New York Press, 21–52.

Dissanayake, Wimal (ed.) (1993) *Melodrama and Asian Cinema*. Cambridge: Cambridge University Press.

_____ (1994) *Colonialism and Nationalism in Asian Cinema*. Bloomington: Indiana University Press.

Eberhard, Wolfram (1950) *A History of China*. London: Routledge & Kegan Paul.

Ebrey, Patricia B. (1991) *Confucianism and Family Rituals in Imperial China: A Social History of Writing about Rites*. Princeton: Princeton University Press.

Eisner, Ken (1993) Review of *The Days*, in Barbara Holton and Frank McDermott (eds) *Variety's Film Reviews 1993–1994*. New Providence: R. R. Bowker, 34.

Elley, Derek (1998) Review of *Mr Zhao*, Variety, 24 August, 29.

_____ (1999a) Review of *Crazy English*, *Variety*, 30 August, 58.

_____ (1999b) Review of *Seventeen Years*, *Variety*, 13 September, 7.

Elsaesser, Thomas (1973) 'Tales of Sound and Fury: Observations on the Family Meldrama', *Monogram*, 4, 2–15.

Evans, Richard (1995) *Deng Xiaoping and the Making of Modern China*. London: Penguin.

Fairbank, John K. (1988) *The Great Chinese Revolution 1800–1985*. London: Chatto & Windus.

Frater, Patrick (1999) 'China tears down Walls for Media', *Screen International*, November 1999, 1.

Garside, Roger (1981) *Coming Alive: China after Mao*. London: Andre Deutsch.

Gledhill, Christine (1987) *Home is Where the Heart is: Studies in Melodrama and the Woman's Film*. London: BFI.

Goldman, Steven (1993) *Sunday Times Magazine*, 26 December, 8.

Goldstein, Alice and Sidney Goldstein (1992) 'Migration in China: Methodological and Policy Challenges', in Dudley L. Poston and David Yaukey (eds) *The Population of Modern China*. New York and London: Plenum Press, 617–632.

Halligan, F. (1994) 'China Syndrome Heats Up', *Screen International*, June 1994, 11.

Hawley, Sandra M. (1991) 'The Importance of Being Charley Chan', in Jonathan Goldstein, Jerry Israel and Hilary Conroy (eds) *America Views China: American Images of China Then and Now*. London and Toronto: Associated University Press, 32–147.

Hilton, Isabel (1981) 'A Hundred Flowers, or Poisonous Weeds', *Index on Censorship*, 10, 4, 16–19.

Hong, Fan (1997) *Footbinding, Fetishism and Freedom: The Liberation of Women's Bodies in Modern China*. London: Frank Cass.

Isaacs, Harold R. (1972) *Images of Asia: American Views of China and India*. New York: Harper & Row.

Iseli, Christian (1997) 'Technical Problems ... a la Chinoise', *Dox: Documentary Film Magazine*, August, 12–13.

Jaschok, Maria and Suzanne Miers (1994) *Women and Chinese Patriarchy: Submission, Servitude and Escape*. Hong Kong: Hong Kong University Press.

Jiao, Xiongping (2001) 'Discussing *Red Sorghum*' in Frances Gateward (ed.) *Zhang Yimou*. University Press of Mississippi, 3–14.

Johnson, Kay A. (1983) *Women, the Family and Peasant Revolution in China*. Chicago: University of Chicago Press.

Jones, Adam M. (1994) Review of *Farewell My Concubine*, The Independent, 7 January, 23.

Jones, David B. (1995) *The Portrayal of China and India on the American Screen 1986–1955*. Cambridge, MA: Massachusetts Institute of Technology.

Kaplan, E. Ann (1991) 'Problematising Cross-Cultural Analysis: The Case of Women in Recent Chinese Cinema', in Chris Berry (ed.) *Perspectives on Chinese Cinema*. London: BFI, 141–54.

Kaplan, E. Ann (1993) 'Melodrama/subjectivity/ideology; Western Melodrama theories and their relevance to recent Chinese cinema', in Wimal Dissanayake (ed.) *Melodrama and Asian Cinema*. Cambridge: Cambridge University Press, 9–28.

Kemp, Philip (1994) Review of *The Blue Kite*, *Sight and Sound*, 4, 2, 55.

Kleinman, Arthur (1986) *Social Origins of Distress and Disease: Depression, Neurasthenia, and Pain in Modern China*. New Haven and London: Yale University Press.

Lee, Leo O. (1991) 'The Tradition of Modern Chinese Cinema: Some Preliminary Explorations and Hypothesis', in Chris Berry (ed.) *Perspectives on Chinese Cinema*. London: BFI, 6–20.

Li, Lu (1990) *Moving the Mountain: My Life in China from the Cultural Revolution to Tiananmen Square*. London: Pan.

Loiseau, Jean-Claude (2001) 'La Dame de Pekin', *Télérama*, 2668, 54–6.

Lopate, Phillip (1994) 'Odd Man Out: Tian Zhuangzhuang interviewed', *Film Comment*, July/August, 60–4.

Lynch, Daniel C. (1999) *After the Propaganda State: Media, Politics and 'Thought Work' in Reformed China*. Stanford: Stanford University Press.

Ma, Ning (1987) 'Notes on Three Chinese Directors', in George S. Semsel (ed.) *Chinese Film: The State of the Art in the People's Republic of China*. New York: Praeger, 63–93.

____ (1988) 'New Chinese Cinema: A Critical Account of the Fifth Generation', *Cinemaya*, Winter, 20–9.

____ (1989) 'Symbolic Representation and Symbolic Violence: Chinese Family Melodramas of the Early 1980s', *East-West Film Journal*, 4, 1, 79–112.

MacBean, James R. (1975) *Film and Revolution*. Bloomington: Indiana University Press.

Mackerras, Colin (1982) *Modern China: a Chronology*. London: Thames & Hudson.

Malcolm, Derek (1994) *The Guardian*, Section 2, 4 October, 2–3.

Mao Tse-Tung (1967) *Selected Readings from the Works of Mao Tse-Tung*. Peking: Foreign Languages Press.

Marshall, Lee (1999) Review of *Seventeen Years*, *Screen International*, 29 October, 20.

Martin, Graham D. (1975) *Language, Truth and Poetry*. Edinburgh: Edinburgh University Press.

Mayfair, Mei-Hui Yang (2001) 'Of Gender, State, Censorship, and Overseas Capital: An Interview with Chinese Director Zhang Yimou', in Frances Gateward (ed.) *Zhang Yimou*. University Press of Mississippi, 35–49.

McDougall, Bonnie S. (1984) *Popular Chinese Literature and Performing Arts in the People's Republic of China 1949–1979*. Berkeley: University of California Press.

McKibbens, Adrienne (1989) 'China's Studio System', *Cinema Papers*, 4 July, 23–4.

Menski, Werner (ed.) (1995) *Coping with 1997: The Reaction of the Hong Kong People to the Transfer of Power*. Stoke-on Trent: Trentham Books.

Moise, Edwin E. (1986) *Modern China: A History*. New York: Longman.

Money, David C. (1990) *China: The Land and The People*. London: Evans Brothers.

Moore-Gilbert, Bart (1997) *Postcolonial Theory: Contexts, Practices, Politics*. London: Verso.

Morris, Mark (2000) *The Observer*, 23 July, 4.

Mulvey, Laura (1975) 'Visual Pleasure and Narrative Cinema', *Screen*, 16, 3, 6–18.

Needham, Robert (1994) 'New Year's Resolution', *The Sunday Times*, Section 9, 9 September, 2–3.

Niogret, Hubert (1994) 'Tian Zhuangzhuang interviewed', *Positif*, 397, 38–42.

Pan, Lynn (1987) *The New Chinese Revolution*. London: Hamish Hamilton.

Petiprez, Veronique (1993) 'Being a Woman in the Films of the Fifth Generation' (Trans. Latika Padgaonkar), *Cinemaya*, Autumn, 32–6.

Pickowicz, Paul G. (1993) 'Melodramatic Representation and the May Fourth Tradition of Chinese Cinema', in Ellen Widmer and David D. Wang (eds) *From May Fourth to June Fourth: Fiction and Film in the Twentieth Century*. Harvard: Harvard University Press, 295–326.

_____ (1994) 'Huang Jianxin and the Notion of Postsocialism', in Nick Browne, Paul G. Pickowicz, Vivian Sobchack and Esther Yau (eds) *New Chinese Cinemas: Forms, Identities, Politics*. Cambridge: Cambridge University Press, 57–87.

Plummer, Mark A. (1991) 'The View from Mao's Tomb', in Jonathan Goldstein, Jerry Israel and Hilary Conroy (eds) *America Views China: American Images of China Then and Now*. London and Toronto: Associated University Press, 210–19.

Poston, Dudley L. and Toni Falbo (1992) 'Effects of the One-Child Policy on the Children of China', in Dudley L. Poston and David Yaukey (eds) *The Population of Modern China*. New York and London: Plenum Press, 427–43.

Pride, Ray (1998) 'New Year's Resolution: interview with Wayne Wang' *Filmmaker*, 6, 3, 68–9.

Purcell, Hugh (1977) *Mao Tse Tung*. Hove: Wayland.

Rayns, Tony (1986) 'Review of *Yellow Earth*', *NFT Monthly Film Bulletin*, October, 295–6.

_____ (1992a) 'Nights at the Opera', *Sight and Sound*, 1, 8, 10–13.

_____ (1992b) 'Interview with Chen Kaige', *Sight and Sound*, 8, 10–13.

_____ (1993) 'Dream On', *Sight and Sound*, 3, 7, 16–19.

_____ (1994) *Time Out*, 5 December, 22.

_____ (1995) 'Review of *The Days*', *Sight and Sound*, 5, 3, 78–9.

_____ (1996) 'Provoking Desire', *Sight and Sound*, 6, 7, 26–9.

_____ (1997) 'The Well Dries Up', *Index on Censorship*, 26, 1, 89–94.

Rayns, Tony and Scott Meek (1980) *BFI Dossier Number 3 Electric Shadows: 45 Years of Chinese Cinema*. London: BFI.

Remy, Vincent (1994) 'Le Cerf-volant Bleu', *Télérama*, 5 February, 28–32.

Reynaud, Berenice (1993) 'Glamour and Suffering: Gong Li and the History of Chinese Stars', *Sight and Sound*, 3, 8, 13.

Rist, Peter and Donato Totaro (2000) 'You've Got Mail!', *Cinemaya*, 47/48, Spring/Summer, 11–15.

Rohdie, Sam (1997) 'The Independence of Form: Report on the 1995 Hong Kong Film Festival', *Pix*, 2, 116–25.

Romney, Jonathon (1994) 'Hooked on Classics', *New Statesman and Society*, 7 January, 33–4.

Rooney, David (1996) Review of *Sons*, *Variety*, 12 February, 21.

Rius & Friends (1980) *Mao for Beginners*. New York: Writers and Readers Publishing.

Said, Edward W. (1979) *Orientalism*. London: Routledge and Kegan Paul.

Schilling, Mark (1993) '*The Blue Kite*', *Screen International*, 12 November, 19.

Segal, Gerald (1993) *The Fate of Hong Kong*. London: Simon & Schuster.

Semsel, George S. (ed.) (1987) *Chinese Film: The State of the Art in the People's Republic*. New York: Praeger.

Semsel, George S., Xu Chen and Xia Hong (1993) (eds) *Film in Contemporary China: Critical Debates 1979–1989*. New York: Praeger.

Shaw, Victor N. (1996) *Social Control in China: A Study of Chinese Work Units*. Westport: Praeger.

Shipp, Steve (1995) *Hong Kong, China: a Political History of the British Crown Colony's Transfer to Chinese Rule*. Jefferson: MacFarland.

Shu, Kai (1993) 'Letter to Chen Kaige', *Cinemaya*, Summer, 18–20.

Sklar, Robert (1994) 'People & Politics, Simple & Direct – an interview with Tian Zhuangzhuang', *Cineaste*, October, 36–8.

Snow, Edgar (1937) *Red Star Over China*. London: Gollancz.

Spence, Jonathan D. (1990) *The Search for Modern China*. New York: Norton.

Spence, Jonathan D. and Annping Chin (1996) *The Chinese Century: The Photographic History of the Last Hundred Years*. London: HarperCollins.

Stacey, Judith (1983) *Patriarchy and Socialist Revolution in China*. Berkeley: University of California Press.

Sun, Shaoyi (2000) 'Under the Shadow of Commercialisation: The Changing Landscape of Chinese Cinema'. Available on-line at: http://www.usc.edu/isd/archives/asianfilm/china/landscape.html

Tang Nin (1993) 'The Pure Artistic Spirit – The famous director Huang Shuqin', *China Screen*, 3, 16–17.

Taylor, Chris (ed.) (1996) *China: A Lonely Planet Survival Kit*. Australia: Lonely Planet Publications.

Tessier, Max (1993) 'Farewell to My Concubine: Art over Politics', *Cinemaya*, 20, 16–18.

Turner, Graham (1988) *Film as Social Practice*. London: Routledge.

Vidal-Hall, Judith (1995) 'History, homage, memory: interview with Tian Zhuangzhuang', *Index on Censorship*, 24, 6, 80–1.

Wakin, Eric (1997) *Asian Independence Leaders*. New York: Facts on File.

Walker, Alexander (1994) 'Review of *Farewell My Concubine*', *The Evening Standard*, 6 January, 30.

Wang, Yuejin (1989) 'The Cinematic Other and the Cultural Self: Decentering the Cultural Identity in Cinema', *Wide Angle*, 11, 2, 32–9.

Wang (1999) 'Review of *Not One Less*', *Cinemaya*, 45, Autumn, 20–1.

Weidmann, Kate (1996) *The Evening Standard*, 11 November, 48.

Whittock, Trevor (1990) *Metaphor and Film*. Cambridge: Cambridge University Press.

Widmer, Ellen and David D. Wang (1993) *From May Fourth to June Fourth: Fiction and Film in the Twentieth Century*. New York: Harvard University Press.

Wilkinson, Kate (2000) *National Film Theatre Programme*, February, 36–7.

Wilson, Dick (1991) *China's Revolutionary War*. London: Weidenfield and Nicholson.

Wollen, Peter (1972) *Signs and Meaning in the Cinema*. London: Secker and Warburg.

Woo, Catherine Y. (1991) 'The Chinese Montage: From Poetry and Painting to the Silver Screen', in Chris Berry (ed.) *Perspectives on Chinese Cinema*. London: BFI, 21–61.

Xu, Ben (1997) '*Farewell My Concubine* and its Nativist Critics', *Quarterly Review of Film and Video*, 16, 2, 155–70.

Yan, Yunxiang (2000) 'Of Hamburgers and Social Space: Consuming McDonald's in Beijing', in Deborah S. Davis (ed.) *The Consumer Revolution in Urban China*. Berkeley: University of California Press, 201–25.

Yau, Esther C. M. (1989) 'Cultural and Economic Dislocations: Filmic Phantasies of Chinese Women in the 1980s', *Wide Angle*, 11, 2, 6–21.

Yao, Xinzhong (2000) *An Introduction to Confucucianism*. Cambridge: Cambridge University Press.

Zha, Jianying (1994) 'Chen Kaige and the Shadows of the Revolution', *Sight and Sound*, 4, 2, 28–36.

Zhang, Yimou (1994) *Big Fish in China*. BBC Video.

Zhao, Henry Y. and John Cayley (eds) (1994) *Under-Sky Underground: Chinese Writing Today*. London: Wellsweep Press.